EUROPEAN PAINTINGS
IN CANADIAN COLLECTIONS
II. MODERN SCHOOLS

PIERRE-AUGUSTE RENOIR: *Claude et Renée*
The National Gallery of Canada
(See page 55)

EDITED
WITH
AN
ESSAY
ON
THE
COLLECTING
OF
MODERN
PICTURES
IN
CANADA

European  Paintings

in
CANADIAN
COLLECTIONS
II. MODERN SCHOOLS

BY
R. H. HUBBARD
CHIEF CURATOR
THE
NATIONAL
GALLERY
OF
CANADA

TORONTO
OXFORD
UNIVERSITY
PRESS
1962

TO THE RIGHT HONOURABLE

VINCENT MASSEY, C.H.

© Oxford University Press, 1962

PRINTED AND BOUND IN ENGLAND BY
HAZELL WATSON AND VINEY LTD
AYLESBURY AND SLOUGH

FOREWORD

It is a source of special satisfaction to me that a second volume should follow the first in the series, *European Paintings in Canadian Collections: Earlier Schools*, which appeared in 1956. Like the first volume, this book constitutes the first publication, apart from exhibition catalogues and a few articles in periodicals, of the nineteenth- and twentieth-century European pictures in Canadian collections. Collecting in this field has greatly accelerated since the Second World War, and many new treasures have been added to the few but distinguished works gathered by our pioneer collectors in the early part of the century. Dr Hubbard has here included works in both private and public collections, for the two are very closely linked with one another. Many of the fine paintings in our museums are the gifts of collectors turned benefactors, and I can only hope that their example will always be followed. Private collectors and museums stimulate each other in many ways, not the least of which are the enthusiasm and sometimes the friendly rivalry which they generate. I trust that this book itself will provide further stimulation and will contribute not only to the spread of knowledge about our national treasures but also to the determination to preserve and enhance our artistic heritage. Finally, I hope that the promise held out in the foreword to the first volume will be fulfilled, that similar books will appear on other fields of our national collecting.

CHARLES F COMFORT
Director

The National Gallery of Canada
December 1961

PREFACE

In this second volume I have tried to gather together the works of the most important European painters of the nineteenth and twentieth centuries that exist in Canadian collections. The first volume listed the paintings from the Continental schools dating before the end of the eighteenth century, but it continued the English school into the nineteenth century far enough to include the works of the two culminating figures of landscape painting, Turner and Constable. In the present volume the Continental schools begin with those painters who, though born in the eighteenth century, worked in the nineteenth; and the British school begins with artists who were actually born in the nineteenth. The volume concludes with artists born just before 1900, for the collecting of contemporary art is too much in flux to be recorded in permanent form.

This book reflects the tastes and preferences of private and public collectors in Canada over a period of some eighty years. French painting, especially the period from Corot to Van Gogh, is well represented. And, as is to be expected, British painting of some periods is covered in a somewhat more minute way than the French. It may be felt that the great flaw in the mirror that this book presents is that it does not record the many Dutch modern pictures which were avidly collected by Canadians in the late nineteenth century. These, however, would have enlarged the book without adding to its quality. The most interesting development in recent years has been the appearance of the German Expressionists and Italian Futurists in our collections. Most of these belong to private collectors who have arrived in Canada since the Second World War.

As in the first volume, there are two parts to this book: the plates at the beginning and the checklist at the end. The plates include what I consider to be the best works of the period in the country, though here I have been somewhat limited by the number I have been able to reproduce. The choice is my own and, though I have benefited from the advice of my colleagues at the National Gallery and Miss Kathleen M. Fenwick in particular, I must take full responsibility for it. As the quality of the individual pictures themselves was my first consideration in making the selection, I could make no real attempt to represent the various collections equally. If the National Gallery of Canada and a few other collections have the preponderance, it is because they have had greater funds with which to acquire pictures.

The checklist comprises all the paintings of the period that are known to me. With the great majority of them I am acquainted at first hand; a few others I know only through reliable publications. I have had to omit others of which I had heard but could not manage to see. Any such list is bound to be incomplete, and this is doubly true in a field in which there is such ardent collecting today. It is my hope that the list as it stands, and the book as a whole, will lead to a fuller publication of our art treasures.

I have included as Europeans a few painters whose nationality is in dispute. Mary Cassatt is included in the French school because she was one of the two women who exhibited with the Impressionists. Two other American-born painters, Whistler and Sargent, appear with the English school because of their close connection with it during most of their lives. The Austrian (or Czech) painter Kokoschka, and the Russian-born Jawlensky and Kandinsky, I have for convenience's sake placed in the German school with which they were associated. For similar reasons the French school (which includes the School of Paris) lists painters born in various parts of Europe.

My thanks are due to the many who in various ways have helped me with this work. The directors of the principal art museums in the country, especially Dr Martin Baldwin of the Art Gallery of Toronto, Mr John Steegman and Dr Evan Turner of the Montreal Museum of Fine Arts, and Dr Ferdinand Eckhardt of the Winnipeg Art Gallery, have been generous with their assistance and have supplied me with photographs of the paintings in their collections. I am also indebted to those who helped me to visit private collections in various cities: Mrs A. C. Matthews and Mrs David Meltzer of Toronto; Mr Murray Vaughan and Mr Edward Cleghorn of Montreal; Mrs Peter Dobell of Ottawa; and Mrs J. L. Shadbolt of Vancouver. Finally, I must thank the private collectors themselves for the courtesies they have extended to me and the photographs they have given me.

R. H. HUBBARD

CONTENTS

COLOUR PLATES

MONOCHROME PLATES

FRENCH SCHOOL

[xiv]

GERMAN SCHOOL

BRITISH SCHOOL

THE COLLECTING OF MODERN
PICTURES IN CANADA

'The lover of art who finds himself in Montreal and proceeds to investigate the art treasures possessed by the energetic inhabitants of that prosperous city will be astonished at the results of his search. He will discover not one or two, but some dozen or more collections of importance. He will see really splendid examples of almost all the chief schools of painting—renaissance and modern. He will find this wealth of pictures possessed by men of action whose time is mostly occupied in handling affairs of public moment, and whose leisure time alone can be bestowed upon the acquirement of the knowledge which the formation of such collections implies. The Montreal collectors are by no means puppets in the hands of dealers; one and all of them choose for themselves. This is emphatically true of Sir William Van Horne.'

These impressions of Sir Martin Conway were recorded in *The Connoisseur* for July 1905.[1] By that time Van Horne (1843-1915), who was one of the chief builders of the Canadian Pacific Railway and a late Victorian of extraordinary vitality, had already acquired most of the older paintings which I listed in the first volume of this book. He had also begun to buy nineteenth-century pictures. Conway, citing only the works of Théodore Rousseau and the painters of Barbizon, remarked of this part of the collection: 'Many other artists are represented by pictures chosen because they pleased the buyer, without regard to made reputations. In all of these is merit; the collector has a definite taste of his own, and buys to satisfy it.'

The truth of the last statement was amply borne out before Van Horne's death ten years later, for he had advanced to the forefront of his generation in matters of taste. His collection included not only the more usual names—Delacroix, Corot, Daubigny—but also Daumier and Courbet, and the French Impressionists who were still in the *avant-garde*. He bought pictures directly from the studios of Pissarro and Renoir. He owned two Cézannes, a Mary Cassatt, a Marie Laurencin, and, perhaps most remarkable of all, two canvases by Toulouse-Lautrec. In addition to these he bought several pictures by the eccentric American genius Albert Pinkham Ryder.

The collection remained intact in the Van Horne house on Sherbrooke Street in Montreal for thirty years after Sir William's death. In 1933, during repairs after a fire, the pictures were exhibited at the Art Association of Montreal (since 1949 called the Montreal Museum of Fine Arts) and drew a record crowd of thirty thousand people. In 1945 that portion of the collection which had been left to Miss Adaline Van Horne, a daughter, went to the Art Association at her bequest. Aside from the important paintings of the earlier schools the highlights of this group were a Delacroix, *Lionne et lion dans leur antre*; an important

---

[1] 'Sir William Van Horne's Collection at Montreal', *Connoisseur*, xii (1905), pp. 135–42. See also Waldmann, 'Modern French Pictures: Some American Collections', *Burlington Magazine*, xvii (1910), pp. 62–66.

Sir William Van Horne (1843–1915)
FROM A DRAWING
Mrs William Van Horne

early Daumier, *Nymphes poursuivies par des satyres*; an exquisite small Renoir of 1881, *Tête de napolitaine*; and an early Cézanne landscape, *La Route à Auvers-sur-Oise.*

In 1946, twenty of the modern pictures left in the collection were sold at Parke-Bernet in New York. In this group, now lost to Canada, were *Christ on the Sea of Gennesaret* by Delacroix, now in the Philadelphia Museum of Art; Daumier's *Le Premier Bain* (Fuchs 52) and *L'Étalage* (Fuchs suppl. 276b); Corot's *Nourrice allaitant* (Robaut 1382); Monet's *La Seine à Bougival*, now in the Smith College Museum; Pissarro's *Old Chelsea Bridge* of 1890; Renoir's beautiful *La Toilette* of 1885 and *Les Sœurs* of 1880–90; Cézanne's *Portrait de Madame Cézanne* (Venturi 520); and the two Lautrecs, *Femme rousse dans le jardin de M. Forest* and *La Gueule de bois.* The latter two fetched $27,500 and $30,000 respectively, and the group as a whole $221,500, high figures for the period. One shudders to think what they would bring today.

Still in the house, where the present Mrs William Van Horne has kindly shown them to me, are a spirited early Daumier, *Les Fugitifs*; a charming small Corot, *La petite curieuse*; a still life which Courbet painted in prison in 1871; a landscape of Louvain by Boudin; and a very early Monet, *The Normandy Coast near Villerville.* There are also works of the Barbizon painters and a host of small pictures by Monticelli, all of which I have recorded here.

Van Horne set the pace for a whole group of rich Montrealers who began collecting at about the same time, but who never matched him in either the quantity or the quality of their holdings. Their collections may be graded on a scale extending from the popular French and Dutch painters at the one extreme to the Impressionists at the other. Writing of this period, A. Y. Jackson, a pioneer of modern painting in Canada, testifies to the Dutch ascendancy in Montreal in a passage of his autobiography that gives little credit to the Van Horne pictures:

'Collectors there had pinned their faith on the Dutch School: the Maris brothers, Mesdag, Israels, Weissenbruch, and others. They boasted that there were more pictures by these artists in Montreal than in any other city in America. The Montreal collectors had been ill-advised; the early collectors had acquired Barbizon paintings, and it would have been logical if they had continued to buy French works, but when French art went impressionistic Montreal buyers dropped it. Instead of purchasing Pissarros, Sisleys, Manets, Cézannes, and Renoirs, they played safe and bought Dutch paintings at high prices. The only artists

EDGAR DEGAS: *Chevaux de courses*
The National Gallery of Canada
(See page 32)

they ignored were Van Gogh and later Mondrian, probably the most important Dutch painters of the past hundred years.

'When I first went to Paris, I was under the impression that Weissenbruch, Mesdag, and company were great artists, since, in Montreal, I had seen little other work. I soon found out that in the art centre of the world they were almost unknown. In Montreal, however, the word had spread that Dutch art was a good investment; besides, to possess a few canvases by these artists gave their owner social prestige. I remember going to a banker's house once to see a Weissenbruch. It was in an elaborate gold frame with a plate glass over it. From the pride with which the owner allowed me to gaze at it, it might have been a Raphael. A few years ago I went to an exhibition of these Dutch paintings. Though the prices had been marked down to a third of what had been paid for them, there were no sales, and the dealer, disgusted, told me that people would not even come to see them. As an investment, the paintings of the Dutch School had proved of little worth. The Montreal investors would have done better to put their money into the canvases of their fellow-townsmen Morrice and Cullen.'[1]

What Jackson wrote did apply to the majority of collectors. It was certainly true of the bulk of the 127 pictures bequeathed to the Art Association of Montreal in 1909 by William and Agnes Learmont. For apart from a few earlier Dutch and English pictures, and single works by Courbet and Daubigny, this collection contained numerous works by French artists like Diaz de la Peña, Decamps, and Henner, and by their Dutch rivals for popularity, the Maris brothers (Willem, Jacob, and Matthys), Josef Israels, and Johannes Bosboom.

The collection of Sir George Drummond (1829–1910), one of the first advisers of the National Gallery of Canada, fell between the two extremes. It consisted of more than two hundred pictures, many of which were by such popular artists of their time as Rosa Bonheur, Jules Dupré, and Ernest Meissonier, reinforced by Géricault, the Barbizon painters, and Monticelli. But the collection had its greater glories. Apart from its Rubens, Rembrandt, Constable, and Turner it contained an important large Corot, *L'Île heureuse*, painted for the vestibule of Daubigny's house at Auvers; two small studies for Daumier's *Le Wagon de troisième classe*; *Chevreuils dans la neige* by Courbet; a superb small Degas, *L'Artiste dans son atelier*, now in the Gulbenkian collection; and works by Whistler, Jongkind, Fantin-Latour, and Forain. The collection was sold at Christie's in 1919, but some of the pictures were bought in by the family, who presented the Corot to the Art Association as a memorial to Sir George Drummond.

Of the other Montreal collections that of Lord Strathcona (1820–1914) was rather conventional except for a much-discussed Turner, *Mercury and Argus*, now in the National Gallery of Canada. Charles Rudolph Hosmer (1851–1927) in addition to his fine group of eighteenth-century English portraits collected the works of Boudin, Courbet, and other modern painters, which now belong to his daughter, Miss Olive Hosmer. Richard Bladworth Angus (1831–1922) supplemented his older paintings with modern works by Delacroix, Bonington, Corot, and Courbet. He also had a taste for some of the English artists popular in his day: William Etty, Sir David Wilkie, and George Frederick Watts. Most of

[1] A. Y. Jackson, *A Painter's Country* (Toronto, 1958), pp. 14–15.

CAMILLE PISSARRO: *Dulwich College*
Collection of Mr and Mrs J. A. MacAulay, Winnipeg
(See page 36)

the Angus pictures are still in Montreal, at the Museum or with members of the family. James Ross (1848–1913), whose collection was sold at Christie's in 1927, counted Rubens, Rembrandt, and Turner among the older masters and Corot, Courbet, and the painters of Barbizon among the modern. He was one of the few in Canada who owned Pre-Raphaelite paintings.

The few art museums that existed in Canada had not yet distinguished themselves by their possessions. Samuel Butler's famous outcry, 'O God, O Montreal!' was occasioned by his finding a plaster cast of the Discobolus relegated to a lumber room in Montreal in 1875. At that time there was not a single public collection in the country. The Art Association of Montreal, founded in 1860, opened its gallery in Phillips Square in 1879 but for many years did little about forming a permanent collection. In 1908 Richard Angus presented it with one of Etty's best-known pictures, *A Bivouac of Cupid*. In 1909 it received the Learmont bequest and organized an exhibition of French art that abounded in works by the popular painters. Of great painters, only Monet's name appeared in the catalogue. But in 1912 the inaugural exhibition of the present building on Sherbrooke Street displayed the cream of the private collections, including some fine Daumiers, Boudins, and French Impressionists then in Montreal. It was not until 1918 that the Art Association itself bought a significant modern painting: *Les Falaises de Pourville*, a shimmering Monet of 1897.

In 1894 a collection of pictures was given to Mount Allison University in the village of Sackville, New Brunswick, by the estate of a philanthropic merchant, John Owens, who

[xxi]

SIR JOHN MILLAIS:
Portrait of the Marquis of Lorne
The National Gallery of Canada

died at Saint John in 1867. These seem to have been chosen by the painter John Hammond, director of the Owens School of Art, which also moved to Sackville. The oils were by indifferent artists—the American impressionist Childe Hassam is one of the few recognizable names among them—but there were some interesting drawings by Horace Vernet, Etty, and Millet. The collection has been supplemented in recent years by paintings and drawings by Millais and Burne-Jones given by Lord Beaverbrook.

In Ontario, the Art Gallery of Hamilton lay dormant for thirty-five years after its founding in 1914. Even the Art Gallery of Toronto, which had opened in 1900, served only as an exhibiting place in the years before the First World War. It is notable at that period mainly for the loan exhibitions which it held of pictures owned privately in Toronto. The Toronto public got its first real taste of modern art in a large exhibition which the French government lent to the Canadian National Exhibition of 1917 as a wartime gesture. Included were such masterpieces as *Le Balcon* by Manet and *L'Estaque* by Cézanne, which were then in the Musée du Luxembourg and are now in the Louvre.

Before the First World War the National Gallery of Canada at Ottawa had only the merest beginnings of a collection. It was founded in 1880 by the Governor-General of the day, the Marquis of Lorne, and his wife the Princess Louise, the artist daughter of Queen Victoria. No doubt it was they who inspired Millais, Watts, and Lord Leighton to make gifts of their own paintings to the Gallery in its first few years.

In 1910, the year of the appointment of the first full-time curator, Eric Brown (1877–1939), the Gallery acquired an impressive landscape by Boudin. The following year it bought Holman Hunt's portrait of *Henry Wentworth Monk*, the Ottawa-born political prophet and friend of the Pre-Raphaelites. The catalogue of 1912 lists these as well as pictures by several modern Dutch painters and a few of the French including Théodore Rousseau and Monticelli. In 1913 and 1914 the Gallery bought pictures by Corot and Millet, an early Sisley, and one of the most 'abstract' of Monet's variations on the famous theme of *Waterloo Bridge*. At the same time there arrived a large batch of English paintings by artists of the calibre of Frank Brangwyn, D. Y. Cameron, and Gerald Kelly. One senses that these were intended to serve as examples to Canadian painters, and if so, their purpose was to be frustrated. For these very years saw the rise of a national movement in art that led to the formation of the Group of Seven—which the Gallery supported from the beginning. Most of the significant English painters of the period unfortunately were not bought, and Sickert, Paul Nash, Augustus John, and Matthew Smith had to wait some years for recognition in Ottawa.

CLAUDE MONET: *Vétheuil en été*
The Art Gallery of Toronto
(See page 44)

The outbreak of war in 1914 brought purchasing to an end, and when the Parliament building was destroyed by fire two years later the National Gallery was forced to vacate its quarters in the Victoria Museum to make room for the legislators. It reopened in 1921. In 1920 the government deposited the numerous works commissioned by Lord Beaverbrook's Canadian War Memorials in the Gallery. These comprised, apart from the many works of Canadian artists, a number of large canvases by such vital English artists as Paul Nash, Wyndham Lewis, William Roberts, and Edward Wadsworth.

Purchasing was resumed after the war and continued at a deliberate pace for the next two decades. In 1921 a large pastel by Degas, *Danseuses à la barre*, set up a new standard of quality for subsequent collecting. A late Pissarro, *Le Pont de Pierre à Rouen*, was bought in 1923 and a good Bonington landscape in 1926. During the economic depression of the thirties, when purchase appropriations were cut to the bone, the Gallery organized a loan exhibition of French painting from Ingres to Seurat in which works from Canadian private collections were set beside fine works supplied by dealers. Some of the latter were bought by collectors, so that the number of modern paintings in the country was increased even if the National Gallery could buy nothing. On the eve of the Second World War the Gallery was able to strengthen its collection by adding a Cézanne of 1875, *Portrait de Boyer*, and a famous early Corot, *Le Pont de Narni*. But in 1940 purchasing was again suspended for the duration of the war.

[xxiii]

Two Ottawa private collections stood out in the thirties by their excellence. Gordon Cameron Edwards (1866–1947), a timber magnate, owned a distinguished group of French pictures that included Daumier's final version of *Le Wagon de troisième classe*; three examples each of Courbet, Pissarro, and Jongkind, and two by Sisley; and single works by Corot, Manet, Renoir, and Cézanne. Some of these (as I have noted below) entered the National Gallery, others were sold, and still others remain with the Edwards heirs in Ottawa. But the best collection of modern French paintings in the country was that of Harry Stevenson Southam (1875–1954), a newspaper publisher and for a long period chairman of the trustees of the National Gallery. Among his earlier pictures Southam owned a fine early portrait by Ingres, *Pierre-François Bernier* (Wildenstein 3) and an excellent Corot, *Cour normande avec deux vaches* (Robaut 403). He also had four Courbets and a Daumier—the concentration on this artist's work is one of the curious facts of private collecting in Canada—as well as works by Monet, Pissarro, Sisley, Redon, and Toulouse-Lautrec. The Post-Impressionists were represented by a small Cézanne, *Portrait du fils de l'artiste* (Venturi 677); two Gauguins of the Brittany period; and two important Van Gogh landscapes, of the Arles and Saint-Rémy periods respectively, *Les Oliviers* (De la Faille 710) and *Paysage sous un ciel mouvementé* (De la Faille 575). Southam recognized more recent developments by his purchase of two paintings by Matisse (one was *Les deux raies* of 1920 now in the Norton Gallery, West Palm Beach); Picasso's *Fruit Dish*, now in the Museum of Modern Art, New York; and pictures by Derain, Modigliani, and Utrillo. Except for the pictures which he presented to the National Gallery and the Art Gallery of Hamilton, the whole collection was sold in New York about 1945.

In Toronto, collections had been formed by a number of private citizens who made gifts and bequests to the Art Gallery of Toronto. One of these was Chester Daniel Massey (1850–1926), who set an example to his son, the Right Hon. Vincent Massey. The latter, while he was High Commissioner for Canada in London from 1935 to 1946, made a comprehensive collection of modern English paintings. Frank Porter Wood (1882–1955) presented one of the several versions of *La Montée au Calvaire*, by Delacroix after Tiepolo, to the Art Gallery in 1930 and at his death left to it several important Old-Master paintings. Wood also owned paintings by Renoir and Berthe Morisot which are still with members of his family in Toronto. Sir Edmund Walker (1848–1924), the first chairman of the National Gallery trustees, collected Japanese prints and a rather conventional group of pictures by Bonington, Daubigny, Harpignies, Monticelli, and the modern Dutch painters.

At the time of the National Gallery's French exhibition of 1934 Mrs Wilmot Matthews of Toronto acquired a fine early ballet scene by Degas, *Danseuse rose*. At about this time also, Dr and Mrs H. M. Tovell were buying choice drawings and paintings by Delacroix, Rouault, and Jacques Villon. Members of the numerous Osler family collected French pictures in Toronto in the earlier part of the century. The late Mrs H. S. Osler of Ottawa owned several Impressionist paintings, and her son Mr Philip Osler of Montreal has recently lent a group of his pictures by Courbet, Boudin, Jongkind, Monet, and Sisley to the Montreal Museum.

Collecting in Montreal lost some of its momentum during the twenties and thirties. The

PIERRE-AUGUSTE RENOIR: *Tête de napolitaine*
The Montreal Museum of Fine Arts
(See page 52)

Art Association acquired a late Pissarro landscape, *Le Port de Rouen*, in 1921, an early Sisley in 1922, and a Courbet landscape in 1925, but little of interest from then until 1937 when it bought a painting by Utrillo. Private collecting was maintained, though not on the scale of the Van Hornes or Drummonds. The personal taste of Elwood B. Hosmer (1879–1946), the son of Charles Hosmer, was for northern European paintings of the Renaissance and the early Canaletto among the older painters. In modern painting he concentrated on the sparkling beach scenes by the early Boudin, and the executors of the Hosmer estate still maintain one of the best collections of these in the world. Hosmer also bought pictures by Delacroix, Corot, and Fantin-Latour. His sister Miss Olive Hosmer has continued the family tradition by adding pictures by Corot and Van Gogh to her collection. Robert Wilson Reford (1867–1951) collected landscapes by Bonington as well as paintings from the older schools. Huntly Redpath Drummond (1864–1957), the son of Sir George Drummond, formed his own collection of modern paintings which included a beautiful late Pissarro, *La grange, matin*, a Sisley, a Renoir, and a Modigliani; these were left to his heirs in Montreal. Mrs I. A. Chipman also began at about this time a well-chosen modern collection that contains pictures by Rouault and Modigliani, a well-known Dufy of the Fauve period (*Les Pêcheurs*), and a very early Fernand Léger.

The state of Montreal collecting just before the Second World War was summed up in the exhibition '19th-Century Landscape Painting' organized by the Art Association in 1939. Concentrating on the French Impressionists and Post-impressionists, it showed that the spell which the lesser and extraneous European painters had so long exerted over the city had finally been broken.

The Art Gallery of Toronto, aided by funds from the Reuben Wells Leonard estate and other sources, made its first important acquisitions between the wars. A Boudin landscape of Bordeaux harbour came as a gift in 1919, but most of the paintings of high quality arrived in the twenties and thirties. The most important of these were an excellent Monet of 1879, *Vétheuil en été*; a Utrillo of the first quality, *La maison de Berlioz*; Renoir's *Portrait de Claude*; two versions of Pissarro's *Printemps, temps gris, Éragny*; and pictures by Sisley and Augustus John. Toronto is also notable for having acquired paintings by Bonnard and Vuillard at this early period for Canada. With Mr Martin Baldwin as director, the Art Gallery began a series of loan exhibitions which have done much to mould the taste of Canadians. The first was the Van Gogh exhibition of 1937.

Collecting had also begun, on a smaller scale, in other cities besides Montreal, Toronto, and Ottawa. The Winnipeg Art Gallery received modest gifts of paintings from its founding members in 1933 but was obliged to wait another twenty-five years for the beginnings of a collection of modern European art. The Vancouver Art Gallery, founded in 1931, sent a delegation to England to choose the nucleus of its permanent collection. The result, in the modern field, was a group of paintings by Etty, Wilkie, Millais, Orpen, Harold Gilman, and other unspectacular British artists.

The post-war period has been by far the most active for art collecting, public and private, since 1900. Existing galleries have enlarged their holdings, new museums have opened, and private collectors have multiplied. The National Gallery of Canada, more generously pro-

PAUL CÉZANNE: *Portrait de paysan*
The National Gallery of Canada
(See page 60)

vided with government funds than ever before, was in a position to set an example to the rest of the country. Its first act after 1945 was to acquire five of the best pictures from the Gordon Edwards collection. The greatest of these was Daumier's famous *Wagon de troisième classe*, which I have already mentioned. Also included were two important paintings by Pissarro, one early and one late, a lively seascape by Monet, and an early landscape by Cézanne. A Courbet of impressive size, *Les Cascades*, was presented by the Edwards family as a memorial to their father. H. S. Southam, during his lifetime, made a number of valuable

AUGUSTUS JOHN:
Portrait of Vincent Massey C.H.
The National Gallery

gifts, comprising in the modern field an unfinished version of Daumier's *L'homme à la corde*, three works by Courbet of which *Les Rochers à Étretat* is the best known, and a landscape of Pont-Aven by Gauguin.

The Massey Collection of English Painting was presented to the National Gallery in 1946, and added to in subsequent years, by the Massey Foundation. Its eighty-eight works afforded a complete survey of developments in British painting in the earlier part of the century and filled a gap in the Gallery's collection that had been left open since 1914 for lack of funds. It includes distinguished examples by Sickert, Steer, Augustus John, Paul Nash, and other painters.

In 1949 the dispersal of a large part of the famous collection of Ambroise Vollard (1867–1939), the Paris art dealer and patron of artists, took place in Ottawa. After Vollard's death in a motor accident this section of the collection had been sent to Lisbon and from there to the United States in 1940. The Royal Navy seized the shipment at Bermuda, probably on suspicion that it had been sent out of France with German connivance, and deposited it at the National Gallery of Canada. After the war the British Admiralty released it to the French authorities, who then awarded it to two sets of claimants. The division was made under the surveillance of Canadian court officials and the staff of the National Gallery. Thus with my colleagues I watched while masses of unframed paintings and drawings by Renoir, Degas, Cézanne, Gauguin, Rouault, Bonnard, Picasso, and others were divided into rough lots and removed by their owners in the space of a day. Many of them have since appeared on the art market in Europe and America and no doubt have brought very high prices. A small part of the collection was exhibited at the National Gallery of Canada in 1950, and from this the Gallery managed to purchase three important pictures: two large canvases from Cézanne's late period, *Forêt* and *Portrait de paysan*, and a powerful Degas pastel, *Chevaux de courses*. At the same time but from another source the Gallery acquired its first Renoir, *Claude et Renée*.

The exciting events of 1949 and 1950 seemed to fire the Canadian government with enthusiasm for art, and in the next five years there followed the purchase of three paintings by Van Gogh, a fifth Cézanne, a group of landscapes from the Fauve period by Braque, Derain, and Vlaminck, and individual works by Bonnard, Chagall, and Graham Sutherland. The real importance of this influx is only to be appreciated if one remembers that the Gallery bought twelve masterpieces of the older schools from the Prince of Liechtenstein's collection at the same time. All this provided a fitting climax to the directorship of Dr H. O. McCurry which began in 1939 and ended in 1955. In the period between 1955 and 1959, when Mr Alan Jarvis was director, the Gallery purchased additional paintings by Derain,

RAOUL DUFY: *Le Port du Havre*
The Art Gallery of Toronto
(See page 84)

Chagall, Sickert, and Sutherland and its first examples of Vuillard, Picasso, and Matisse. Matisse himself had designated for the Gallery a well-known canvas of 1926, *Nu au canapé jaune*, when the former assistant director, Mr Donald Buchanan, visited him in Paris in 1950. Under Dr Charles Comfort, who was appointed director shortly before the opening of the new National Gallery building in 1960, new plans were made to increase purchase funds and to add substantially to the permanent collection.

Of recent years the art museums of Canada have begun to survey the country's art treasures in a consistent way. This they have done by means of a series of loan exhibitions that have recognized both public and private collections. Thus in 1954 the National Gallery, the Art Gallery of Toronto, and the Montreal Museum of Fine Arts organized the exhibition 'European Masters in Canadian Collections' which embraced both the older and the modern schools. The Art Gallery of Toronto holds exhibitions almost annually to record the accessions of collectors in its region. The Montreal Museum celebrated its centenary in 1960 with the exhibition 'Canada Collects'. Fifty-four collections were represented here, and a number of paintings were borrowed back which had been sold outside the country. In the same year the Winnipeg Art Gallery organized a similar exhibition which summarized the state of collecting there.

The Montreal Museum began its post-war phase auspiciously with the receipt of Miss Adaline Van Horne's bequest of old and modern pictures. This important group at once

GRAHAM SUTHERLAND:
Portrait of Lord Beaverbrook
The Lord Beaverbrook Art Gallery, Fredericton

raised the Museum's collection to a position of international importance and provided it with a basis on which to build further. In the intervening years it has acquired, by gift and purchase, works by Daumier, Renoir, Cézanne, Matisse, Derain, and a number of English contemporary artists. The Art Gallery of Toronto's recent accessions have likewise enhanced its collection. Figure paintings by Ingres, Courbet, Degas, and Renoir, and a Fauve landscape by Dufy among the French, and works by Sickert, Paul Nash, Graham Sutherland, and Ben Nicholson among the English are the highlights of this group. In 1959, however, a setback came with the theft of the Gallery's most valuable paintings, among them the *Portrait de Claude* by Renoir. All were fortunately recovered, though in a damaged condition.

The Art Gallery of Hamilton was also the victim of theft, in April 1960. It lost all the European paintings which H. S. Southam had given it in 1951 as the nucleus of a permanent collection: a Courbet landscape, a fine portrait by Fantin-Latour, and a still life by Braque. (It was this gift that had stimulated a civic movement leading to the erection of a new gallery building in 1953.) I have included the Southam pictures in my lists in the hope that they will soon be recovered. Apart from them the Art Gallery of Hamilton has made other acquisitions by gift and purchase, including paintings by Marquet and Sickert.

The Winnipeg Art Gallery, though still in temporary quarters in the Civic Auditorium, has a modern collection in the process of formation, thanks to the pictures which Mr J. A. MacAulay and his fellow collectors have presented. The modern foreign sections of the Vancouver Art Gallery, the Art Gallery of Victoria, and the new Lord Beaverbrook Art Gallery at Fredericton appear at present to be specializing in the work of British painters— a sensible enough policy in view of the high prices of French pictures. The British collection of the Beaverbrook Gallery culminates in an impressive group of portraits by Graham Sutherland, including a highly expressive one of the donor himself.

Private collecting has increased a hundredfold in the prosperous years since the war. Some of the initial impetus was given by collectors who were newly arrived from abroad. The war brought to Canada such discerning Europeans as Mr L. V. Randall of Montreal, whose collection includes rare drawings by older masters and some moderns like Paul Klee. Another was Dr William Landmann of Toronto who owns important examples by the German Expressionists as well as works by Léger and Chagall. The late Hugo Simons brought to Montreal a set of portraits by Otto Dix, and Mr Oskar Federer fine pictures by Corot, Monet, and Renoir. Another arrival was Mr Frederick Mendel, who with characteristic energy built up simultaneously a meat-packing industry and a collection of art in Saskatoon. His pictures represent the School of Paris (Braque, Vlaminck, Dufy, Chagall)

PABLO PICASSO: *Le Guéridon*

The National Gallery of Canada

(See page 99)

MARC CHAGALL: *Au-dessus de Vitebsk*
Collection of Mr and Mrs Samuel Zacks, Toronto
(See page 103)

GEORGES BRAQUE: *Le Port d'Anvers*
The National Gallery of Canada
(See page 92)

and the modern German school (Corinth, Franz Marc, Kirchner, Nolde, and Schmidt-Rottluff).

Montreal maintains its position of importance through the efforts of a group of collectors who have arisen mainly since the war. Among them are Dr and Mrs G. R. McCall, Mr and Mrs Murray Vaughan, Mr and Mrs Maxwell Cummings, and the late Lawrence Porter (of St Andrews East). Mr and Mrs Samuel Bronfman and members of their family have bought choice works by Degas, Pissarro, Renoir, and Redon. Mr and Mrs Lazarus Phillips and their son Mr Ivan Phillips have in a short time amassed an important collection that includes an outstanding Monet of 1882, *Les Rochers de Pourville*; a very early Matisse, *Nature morte au purro* of 1904; a Picasso of the Negro Period; and paintings by Manet, Degas, Sisley, Redon, Van Gogh, Braque, and many others.

The role of Canada's few art dealers in the formation of the country's collections is not to be forgotten. The Watson Galleries, which recently closed in Montreal on the retirement of Mr William Watson, and the Laing Gallery in Toronto, have for many years held annual exhibitions of modern European paintings. The works have been supplied mainly by Van Wisselingh and Company of Amsterdam, whose connection with Canada goes back to the early part of the century. During the Second World War Dr Max Stern arrived in Montreal and opened the Dominion Gallery. Besides encouraging the sales of Canadian art he has also helped to make Canadians conscious of a wider range of foreign art.

Toronto too has numerous collectors. The most vigorous are Mr and Mrs Samuel Zacks, whose holdings are beginning to assume the proportions of a museum. The French section of their collection contains five paintings by Picasso from various periods and four by Matisse. They have several well-known oils by Dufy, a Bonnard of mural size, a large Fauve landscape by Derain, two famous Chagalls, an early Modigliani, and works by Degas, Rouault, Vlaminck, Braque, Léger, and Juan Gris. They have broken new ground in Toronto by their purchase of paintings by the Italian Futurists and of other artists like Paul Klee and Jawlensky. Mr and Mrs John David Eaton have acquired a good still life by Braque from 1938 and examples of Rouault, Bonnard, and some of the painters of today. Mr and Mrs David Meltzer have a harmonious group that includes Degas, Mary Cassatt, Derain, Matisse, Rouault, and Picasso. Mr and Mrs D. M. Dunlap own a Picasso of the Blue Period as well as paintings by Sisley, Utrillo, and Modigliani. Mr and Mrs T. M. Sterling own works by Rouault and Modigliani, the latter a fine portrait, *Jeanne Hébuterne*. In quite another field Colonel and Mrs W. E. Phillips have collected at least a dozen paintings by Augustus John.

In Hamilton, Mr Herman Levy is forming a collection which reflects a discerning taste and now includes a good example of Monet's *Waterloo Bridge* series and works by Pissarro, Marquet, Van Gogh, Utrillo, and Sickert. In Ottawa, Mr and Mrs Hamilton Southam own a beautiful Picasso of 1903, *Femme assise*, bought from the Vollard exhibition of 1950, and other paintings by Renoir, Gauguin, and Rouault.

In western Canada, Winnipeg stands out by virtue of Mr J. A. MacAulay's collection. Its stature today is indicated by the presence of four Van Goghs, a Cézanne landscape, and fine representative works by Corot, Redon, Fantin-Latour, the French Impressionists, the

PAUL NASH: *Solstice of the Sunflower*
The National Gallery of Canada
(See page 140)

AMEDEO MODIGLIANI: *Beatrice Hastings in a Wicker Chair*
Collection of Mr and Mrs Samuel Zacks, Toronto
(See page 111)

Fauves, Bonnard, Vuillard, and many others. In Vancouver, Mrs James Fell has a growing collection of French and English pictures, and Mr and Mrs Thomas Ingledow possess that rarity in Canada, a townscape by Kokoschka.

Finally, there is a growing number of collectors in various parts of the country who concentrate on the art of today. The Art Gallery of Toronto sets an example to the other museums in the serious collecting of contemporary foreign art and is alone in Canada in allowing the public to see examples of modern American art. However, as painters born after the turn of the century do not fall within the scope of the present volume, their works must wait until they are numerous enough to supply the material for another volume in the series.

FRENCH SCHOOL

including the School of Paris

FRENCH SCHOOL

JEAN-BAPTISTE-CAMILLE COROT 1796-1875

Le Pont de Narni

THE NATIONAL GALLERY OF CANADA

In the nineteenth century the most widely known landscape painter before the Impressionists was Corot. He was born in Paris, the son of a wig-maker. After his schooling at Rouen and Passy he returned to Paris where he worked in a draper's shop. He inherited a small income which enabled him to study with two minor landscape artists, Achille Michallon and Victor Bertin. He then began to paint landscapes at Fontainebleau and Ville d'Avray. In 1825 he made his first trip to Italy and spent most of his time in Rome, until his return to Paris in 1828. Between 1828 and 1834 he painted widely in France, and he paid short visits to Italy in 1834 and 1843. Thereafter, except for occasional trips abroad, he painted mostly in the Forest of Fontainebleau. By the eighteen-fifties his work had been widely accepted and he became a very prolific painter. He was a good-hearted man who helped several of his fellow artists when they were in difficulties. He died in Paris.

Le Pont de Narni is the first picture sent by Corot to the Salon in Paris (in 1827) and is a masterpiece of his early style. He painted it in Rome, and the sketch which he made for it is in the Louvre. A drawing of Corot's bedroom made at the time of his death (reproduced in Robaut, i, pp. 324-5) shows what appears to be this picture hanging over the bed. It is a good example of his early clarity of form, classical breadth of composition, and limpidity of colour. Above all, it shows the sensitive and beautiful handling of light that is characteristic of his early career.

Oil on canvas, $26\frac{3}{4}'' \times 37\frac{1}{4}''$.

LITERATURE

Robaut, *Corot* (1905), ii, p. 70, No. 199, reprod. p. 71.
Hamel, *Corot* (1905), Pl. i.
Thieme-Becker, *Allgemeines Lexikon der bildenden Künstler*, vii (1924), p. 451.
Bénézit, *Dictionnaire*, i (1924), p. 1011.
Moreau-Nélaton, *Corot* (1924), pp. 19–20.
Fosca, *Corot* (1930), Pl. 9.
Venturi, *Peintres modernes* (1941), p. 143, reprod.
Bazin, *Corot* (1942), p. 37.
Venturi, *Painters and Painting* (1946), p. 141.
Magazine of Art, xxxix (1946), reprod. p. 372.
Malraux, *Musée imaginaire* (1947), p. 67, reprod. p. 68.
Huyghe, *Dialogue avec le visible* (1955), p. 213, Pl. 197.
Baud-Bovy, *Corot* (1957), p. 79.
Canaday, *Mainstreams of Modern Art* (1959), p. 126, reprod. p. 125.
Fosca, *Corot* (1958), pp. 19–20.
Hubbard, *National Gallery of Canada Catalogue*, ii (1959), pp. 12-13, reprod.

EXHIBITED

Paris, Salon of 1827, No. 221.
Paris, *Centenaire Corot*, 1895, No. 116.
Toronto, Art Gallery, *Great Paintings*, 1940, No. 89.
Montreal, Art Association, *Masterpieces*, 1942, No. 54.
New York Wildenstein, *Corot*, 1942, No. 9.
Philadelphia, Museum, *Corot*, 1946, No. 6, reprod. in cat.
St Louis, City Art Museum, *40 Masterpieces*, 1947, No. 8, reprod. in cat.
Toronto, Canadian National Exhibition, 1949, No. 129.
Philadelphia, Museum, *Diamond Jubilee*, 1950, No. 56, reprod. in cat.
Venice, Biennale, 1952, *Corot*, No. 2, reprod. in cat.
Toronto, Art Gallery, &c., *European Masters*, 1954, No. 46, reprod. in cat.
Fort Worth, Museum, *Inaugural*, 1954, No. 14.

EX COLLECTION

(*Vente Corot*, Paris, 1875, No. 21.)
Lemaistre.
Charles André (sale, 1893, No. 3).
Desfossés (sale, 1899, No. 16).
Acquired by the National Gallery of Canada, 1940.

[3]

FRENCH SCHOOL

JEAN-BAPTISTE-CAMILLE COROT 1796-1875

L'Île heureuse

THE MONTREAL MUSEUM OF FINE ARTS

Because of its poetic title, evening illumination, and hazy foliage, *L'Île heureuse* epitomizes the style of Corot's later period. Painted about 1864, it is one of a series Corot did for the house of his artist-friend, Charles-François Daubigny, at Auvers-sur-Oise. Another picture by Corot, a small landscape in the National Gallery collection, was painted on the road near Daubigny's house. *L'Île heureuse* once belonged to Sir George Drummond in Montreal; at the sale of his famous collection in London in 1919 it was bought by his family and presented to the Art Association of Montreal. A pendant to this picture, *Don Quixote and Sancho Panza*, is in the Cincinnati Museum.

Oil on canvas, 73″ × 55½″.

LITERATURE

Robaut, *Corot* (1905), iii, p. 152, No. 1644, reprod. p. 153.
Waldmann, *Burlington Magazine*, xvii (1910), pp. 62–5.
Burlington Magazine, xcvii (1955), p. 100.
Montreal Museum of Fine Arts, *Catalogue* (1960), p. 57.

EXHIBITED

Montreal, Art Association, *Loan Exhibition*, 1898.
Montreal, Museum, *6 Centuries of Landscape*, 1952, No. 44, reprod. in cat.

Paris, Orangerie, *Van Gogh et les peintres d'Auvers*, 1954, No. 23.
Montreal, Museum, *Canada Collects*, 1960, No. 27, reprod. in cat.

EX COLLECTION

Charles-François Daubigny, Auvers-sur-Oise.
Sir George Drummond, Montreal (sale, Christie's, London, 26 June, 1919, No. 18). Presented to the Art Association of Montreal by the family of Sir George Drummond in memory of Arthur Lenox Drummond and Lieutenant Guy M. Drummond, 1919.

II

III

HONORÉ DAUMIER 1808-1879

Les Fugitifs

COLLECTION OF MRS WILLIAM VAN HORNE, D.M.G., MONTREAL

Daumier was the greatest caricaturist of the nineteenth century as well as an important Realist painter. He was born in Marseille, the son of a picture-framer. In 1816 his family moved to Paris, where he worked in the law-office and the bookshop which gave him the material for his later caricatures of lawyers and bibliophiles. He had some drawing lessons from Alexandre Lenoir, an admirer of Rubens and Titian, and for a time studied painting with Eugène Boudin. From 1825 to 1830 he was apprenticed to a lithographer, and around 1830 he published his own first lithographs as illustrations for the periodical *La Caricature*. At this time too he was studying Rubens and Goya in the Louvre. In 1832 he was imprisoned for a caricature he had made of Louis-Philippe. In 1835 he joined the staff of *Charivari*, for which he made many illustrations. His lithographs won him the approval of Balzac, Baudelaire, Delacroix, and other writers and painters. He began painting subjects from everyday life about 1835, but as a painter he was not fully recognized until after his death. Strongly opposed to the régime of Napoleon III, he was in disfavour during the Second Empire and so welcomed the Commune of 1871. By 1864 he was in real financial difficulties and soon after 1870 he became blind—the helpful Corot had to rescue him from abject poverty. He died at Valmondois.

This small but powerful picture was painted in 1848 or 1849 and shows Daumier's reaction to the revolution of 1848. General Cavaignac, the military dictator, had ruthlessly crushed the Socialists and arrested about fifteen thousand people. By the end of 1848 the prisons were full and some four thousand of these rebels were deported to Algeria. Under a wintry sky, in the wind and the rain, the refugees plod along a bleak road: it is a tragedy that has often been repeated in subsequent history. Daumier painted it with such passion and movement that the picture was also called 'Le Coup de vent'. The frieze-like composition, the impressionistic treatment of the figures, and the greenish-blue chord of colours are a prophecy of Manet's racing scenes of the sixties.

Oil on panel, $6\frac{1}{4}'' \times 12\frac{1}{4}''$.

LITERATURE

Klossowski, *Daumier* (1908), p. 22.
Fuchs, *Der Maler Daumier* (1927), p. 49, Pl. 84.
Adhémar, *Daumier* (1954), reprod. in colour, Pl. 45.

EXHIBITED

Montreal, Art Association, *Van Horne Collection*, 1933, No. 143.

EX COLLECTION

Béguin.
(*Vente Daumier*, Paris, 1878, No. 17.)
Auguste Boulard (sale, Paris, 1900, No. 107).
Sir William Van Horne, Montreal.

HONORÉ DAUMIER 1808-1879

Nymphes poursuivies par des satyres

THE MONTREAL MUSEUM OF FINE ARTS

This mythological subject from Daumier's early period, painted in 1849 or 1850, is a rare example of his treatment of academic themes. There is, however, nothing conventional about its style. The figures show a vigour and sense of movement that are proof of his study of Rubens. But the most remarkable feature of the picture is the excitement produced by the staccato brushstrokes in the background, which give a foretaste of Van Gogh's expressionist technique. The picture was bought by Sir William Van Horne in 1910 and was bequeathed by his daughter Miss Adaline Van Horne to the Montreal Museum of Fine Arts.

Oil on canvas, $51\frac{3}{4}'' \times 38\frac{1}{2}''$.

LITERATURE

Vignon, *Salon de 1850* (1850), p. 129.
Klossowski, *Daumier* (1908), No. 17.
Van Wisselingh & Co., *Half a Century of Picture Dealing* (1923), No. 6.
Fuchs, *Der Maler Daumier* (1927), p. 51, Pl. 143b.
Art News (4 Nov. 1933), p. 15.
Bourgeois, *Art News* (15–28 Feb. 1942), p. 34, reprod. p.22.
Canadian Art, v (1948), p. 118.
Adhémar, *Daumier* (1954), reprod. in colour, Pl. 56.
Montreal Museum of Fine Arts, *Catalogue* (1960), p. 60.

EXHIBITED

Paris, Salon of 1850, No. 726.
Montreal, Art Association, *Van Horne Collection*, 1933, No. 139.
Montreal, Art Association, *Masterpieces*, 1942, No. 56.
Fort Worth, Art Centre, *Inaugural,* 1954, No. 16, reprod. in cat.
Montreal, Museum, *Canada Collects*, 1961, No. 67.
London, Tate Gallery, *Daumier,* 1961, No. 5, reprod. in cat.

EX COLLECTION

Sir William Van Horne, Montreal (1910).
Bequest of Miss Adaline Van Horne to the Art Association of Montreal, 1945.

IV

V

HONORÉ DAUMIER 1808–1879

Le wagon de troisième classe

THE NATIONAL GALLERY OF CANADA

'The Third-Class Carriage' is one of Daumier's most famous subjects. An unfinished version of it is in the Metropolitan Museum, New York, and a water-colour study for the composition is in the Walters Art Gallery, Baltimore. The National Gallery picture is the final canvas. Here may be seen to best advantage Daumier's skill as a draughtsman and the calligraphic quality of his technique of painting, as well as his dramatic use of lights and shadows. It was painted about 1862, during the upsurge of popular democracy in Europe, and expresses a deep sympathy with the common people and their lot. The sombre note which it sounds echoes Daumier's own plight during the years when he was suffering extreme poverty. The picture was bought by the National Gallery from the well-known collection of the late Gordon C. Edwards of Ottawa.

Oil on canvas, $26\frac{3}{4}'' \times 36\frac{1}{4}''$.

LITERATURE

Klossowski, *Daumier* (1908), p. 18, No. 252.
Les Arts, No. 81 (Sept. 1908), reprod. p. 7.
Thieme-Becker, *Allgemeines Lexikon der bildenden Künstler*, viii (1913), p. 436.
Fontainas, *Daumier* (1923), p. 28, Pl. 12.
Escholier, *Daumier* (1923), reprod. p. 145.
Apollo, iv (1926), reprod. p. 63.
Fuchs, *Der Maler Daumier* (1927), p. 47, Pl. 43.
Waldmann, *Kunst des Realismus und Impressionismus* (1927), p. 628, Pl. 409.
Bertram, *Daumier* (1929), Pl. xiv.
The Arts, xvii (1930), reprod. p. 89.
Mongan, *Gazette des Beaux-Arts*, 6ᵉ pér., xvii (1937), p. 251.
Lassaigne, *Daumier* (1939), Pl. 123.
Burlington Magazine, lxxii (1938), reprod. opp. p. 280.
Marceau and Rosen, *Journal of the Walters Art Gallery*, iii (1940), pp. 15 ff., Pl. 13.
Canadian Art, ii (1945), p. 82, reprod.; iv (1947), p. 124.
Art Quarterly, x (1947), reprod. p. 226.
Studio, cxli (1951), reprod. p. 167.
Adhémar, *Daumier* (1954), pp. 52, 128.
Hubbard, *National Gallery of Canada Catalogue*, ii (1957), pp. 17–18, reprod.

EXHIBITED

Paris, Exposition Universelle, 1889, *Peinture française*, No. 230.
Paris, École des Beaux-Arts, *Daumier*, 1901, No. 43.
Geneva, 1914.
Zurich, Künstlergesellschaft, *Art français*, 1917, No. 78.
London, Tate Gallery, 1924, 1926.
London, Lefevre Gallery, *Daumier*, 1927.
Amsterdam, Van Wisselingh & Co., *Peinture française*, 1928, No. 19, reprod. in cat.
New York, Museum of Modern Art, *Corot-Daumier*, 1930, No. 67.
Ottawa National Gallery, &c., *French Painting*, 1934, No. 40, reprod. in cat.
Montreal, Art Association, *Masterpieces*, 1942, No. 55.
Toledo, Art Museum, &c., *Spirit of Modern France*, 1946, No. 29.
Pittsburgh, Carnegie Institute, *Everyday Life*, 1954, No. 75, reprod. in cat.
London, Tate Gallery, *Daumier*, 1961, No. 69, reprod. in cat.

EX COLLECTION

(*Vente Daumier*, Durand-Ruel, Paris, 1878, No. 62.)
Brame.
Pillet (1882).
Comte Doria (sale, Paris, May 1889, No. 127).
Gallimard, Paris (1901).
Sir James Murray (sale, Knoedler, London, 1927, No. 37).
Gordon C. Edwards, Ottawa.
Acquired by the National Gallery of Canada, 1946.

HONORÉ DAUMIER 1808-1879

Les Amateurs

THE MONTREAL MUSEUM OF FINE ARTS

This fine watercolour, dated by Adhémar between 1856 and 1865, shows Daumier's interest in the expressions of those who look at pictures. A group of art lovers examining paintings in a private collection or in a dealer's gallery presents an amusing variety of types: the authoritative viewer, the bemused spectator, the scrutinizer, the indifferent—all of whom may be found among the visitors to any museum today.

Watercolour, on paper, 14″ × 17¾″.

LITERATURE
Adhémar, *Daumier* (1954), reprod. in colour, Pl. 93.

EXHIBITED
Ottawa, National Gallery, *French Painting*, 1934, No. 41.
Montreal, Art Association, *Masterpieces of Painting*, 1942, No. 57.

Montreal, Museum, *Montreal Collections*, 1949, No. 17.

EX COLLECTION
G. W. Frothingham, Montreal.
W. R. Miller, Montreal.
Presented to the Montreal Museum of Fine Arts in 1951 by Mrs W. R. Miller in memory of her husband.

VI

VII

FRENCH SCHOOL

GUSTAVE COURBET 1819-1877

Les Rochers à Étretat

THE NATIONAL GALLERY OF CANADA

Courbet and Daumier were the greatest painters of the Realist movement in Europe. Courbet, the son of a landowner, was born at Ornans (Doubs) and had his first art lesson there, continuing his studies at Besançon under Charles Flajoulet. By 1840 he was in Paris and had decided to be a painter. Although he studied briefly at the Atelier Suisse with Carl von Steuben and Alexandre Hesse, he later claimed to be self-taught. In 1840 and 1841 he copied the Venetian painters and Velasquez, Frans Hals, and Rembrandt in the Louvre. In his style he soon evolved a vigorous naturalism which he applied to a wide range of subjects. His art first attracted public attention in 1855 when he held a private showing at the Paris Exposition, where the famous *Enterrement à Ornans* and *L'Atelier* created a scandal by their supposedly crude realism. By the eighteen-sixties he was friendly with Boudin, Renoir, Manet, and Whistler. He was at the height of his fame when he joined the Commune of 1871 and was arrested for complicity in the overturning of the Vendôme column in Paris. He was fined and imprisoned, and in 1873 went into voluntary exile in Switzerland. He died at La Tour de Peilz near Vevey.

Because of its wonderful clarity of light and colour *Les Rochers à Étretat* of 1866 is one of Courbet's finest landscapes. It shows his close observation of nature, the strength of his compositions, and his vigorous use of the palette knife to give texture to the paint. In his early period, Pissarro, and through him Cézanne, were influenced by these aspects of Courbet's style. The cliffs at Étretat on the Normandy coast were to become one of Monet's favourite painting places.

Oil on canvas, 36″ × 45″.

LITERATURE
Art News (27 April 1929), reprod. p. 11.
La Biennale di Venezia, Nos. 19–20 (1954), reprod. p. 10.
Hubbard, *National Gallery of Canada Catalogue*, ii (1959), p. 15, reprod.

EXHIBITED
Amsterdam, Van Wisselingh & Co., *Peinture française*, 1929, No. 11, reprod. in cat.

Ottawa, National Gallery, &c., *French Painting*, 1934, No. 34.
Venice, Biennale, 1954, *Courbet*, No. 31, reprod. in cat.
Toronto, Art Gallery, &c., *European Masters*, 1954, No. 53.

EX COLLECTION
H. S. Southam, Ottawa.
Gift of H. S. Southam to the National Gallery of Canada, 1947.

GUSTAVE COURBET 1819-1877

Dans le bois: neige

THE NATIONAL GALLERY OF CANADA

This is one of Courbet's fine snow landscapes, a subject which is rare in European painting, and may be regarded as a forerunner of the winter landscapes of the Canadian school in the twentieth century. Courbet's great contribution to painting in the nineteenth century was a strength and freedom of style, very evident in this picture. The paint is broadly applied with the palette knife—perhaps to get round the problem of drawing, which was his weak point—and by this means he was able to give his pictures a richness of light and shade and an earthy, solid texture which no one had achieved before him. The broad planes serve as a foil for the simple geometrical forms of the trees and house. Courbet thus pointed the way not only towards the Impressionists' use of paint alone to indicate space but also towards the remoter goal of abstraction.

Oil on canvas, $23\frac{1}{2}'' \times 29''$.

LITERATURE
Hubbard, *National Gallery of Canada Catalogue*, ii (1959), p. 16, reprod.

EXHIBITED
Amsterdam, Van Wisselingh & Co., *Peinture française*, 1929, No. 12, reprod. in cat.

Ottawa, National Gallery, &c., *French Painting*, 1934, No. 35.

EX COLLECTION
H. S. Southam, Ottawa.
Presented by H. S. Southam to the National Gallery of Canada, 1950.

VIII

IX

FRENCH SCHOOL

EUGÈNE BOUDIN 1824–1898

Sur la plage à Trouville

ESTATE OF THE LATE ELWOOD B. HOSMER, MONTREAL

Boudin, one of the immediate precursors of the Impressionists, was born at Honfleur, the son of a ship's pilot. He worked as a cabin boy in 1834 and later in a stationer's shop at Le Havre. Here, by 1844, he had set up a framer's shop, where he met Millet and Troyon of the Barbizon School of landscape painters. On their advice he turned to painting, and the town council of Le Havre gave him a scholarship to study in Paris. In the development of his style he was influenced also by Corot and Jongkind. He returned to Le Havre in 1854, and about 1857 began to paint in the open air. He did most of his painting in France at Le Havre, Honfleur, Bordeaux, Trouville, and Deauville, but he also travelled to Belgium, Holland, and Venice. Courbet and Whistler visited him at Trouville in 1865. He admired Manet, but though he exhibited in the first Impressionist exhibition in 1874 he remained outside the circle of the Impressionists. He deeply influenced the young Monet. He died at Deauville and was buried in Paris.

Most sought-after today of all Boudin's works are his sparkling impressions of the beach at Trouville. This example, dated 1864, shows the characteristic jewel-like facets of red and blue in the costumes that give the picture its festive air and its great charm. The composition of the figures and the bathing huts appears to be almost accidental, but in reality it is a very careful construction; this aspect of Boudin's style prefigures important later developments in French painting.

Oil on canvas, 26″ × 40″.

EXHIBITED
Paris, Salon of 1884.
Paris, École des Beaux-Arts, *Boudin*, 1899.
Ottawa, National Gallery, &c., *French Painting*, 1934, No. 1, reprod. in cat.

Montreal, Museum, *Montreal Collections*, 1949, No. 4.
Montreal, Museum, *Six Centuries of Landscape*, 1952, No. 48, reprod. in cat.
Montreal, Museum, *Canada Collects*, 1960, No. 91.

EX COLLECTION
Elwood B. Hosmer, Montreal.

JEAN-FRANÇOIS MILLET 1814–1875

Œdipe détaché de l'arbre

THE NATIONAL GALLERY OF CANADA

Millet, who became famous for his paintings of peasant subjects and for his expression of the 'poetry of toil', was born on a farm near Gréville (Manche). He had his first lessons from several minor artists in the town of Cherbourg, which in 1837 gave him a scholarship to study painting with Delaroche in Paris. For a few years after he returned to Cherbourg he painted portraits and pastoral scenes in the manner of the eighteenth-century French masters. But after going to Paris a second time in 1842 he was decisively influenced by Daumier and turned to the Realist style of painting. His first popular success came with a canvas of 1848, *The Winnower*. The following year he settled in the village of Barbizon in the Forest of Fontainebleau, where he stayed for the rest of his life.

The *Oedipus* is one of Millet's rare mythological subjects. It is an early work, painted in 1847 over another picture, a 'St Jerome in the Desert'. There is a drawing for the figure of Oedipus (see *Corot and Millet*, 1902, Pl. M35). This painting was one of the important early acquisitions of the National Gallery.

Oil on canvas, 52½″ × 20½″.

LITERATURE
Sensier, *Millet* (1881), pp. 68–72, reprod. p. 69.
Souillé, *Millet* (1900), pp. 60–2.
Thomson, *Barbizon School* (1902), p. 222, reprod.
Brown, *Studio*, xliv (1915), p. 206.
Moreau-Nélaton, *Millet* (1921), pp. 61 ff.

EXHIBITED
Paris, Salon of 1847.
Paris, *Millet*, 1877, No. 8.
Paris, Exposition Universelle, 1889, *Peinture française*, No. 514.
Dublin, Irish International Exhibition, 1907.

Montreal, Art Association, 1916.
Toronto, Art Gallery, *Paintings from the National Gallery of Canada*, 1919, No. 53.
Pittsburgh, Carnegie Institute, *Paintings from the National Gallery of Canada*, 1919, No. 58.
Ottawa, National Gallery, *French Painting*, 1934, No. 74.
Winnipeg, Art Gallery, *Pre-impressionist Painters*, 1954, No. 45.

EX COLLECTION
Bodmer (1847–69).
Faure (sale, Paris, 1873).
Édouard Otlet (1889).
G. N. Stevens.
Acquired by the National Gallery of Canada, 1914.

X

FRENCH SCHOOL

HENRI FANTIN-LATOUR 1836–1904

Féerie

THE MONTREAL MUSEUM OF FINE ARTS

Fantin-Latour was born at Grenoble. His father, a pastellist, was his first teacher. From 1850 to 1854 he worked with a local painter, Lecoq de Boisbaudran, then went to Paris and studied at the École des Beaux-Arts. In 1861 he was working in Courbet's studio. He travelled in England, where he became acquainted with the Pre-Raphaelite painters, and in Belgium. Whistler, who knew him well, is said to have envied him his solid knowledge of the craft of painting. He was friendly also with Manet and was always closely associated with the Impressionists, though his style was considerably different from theirs. A romantic imagination and a passion for music led him to paint a number of romantically conceived figure-pieces. His many flower paintings and occasional portraits were done in a much more naturalistic way. He died at Buré (Orne).

This fantasy, painted in 1863, is one of Fantin-Latour's best-known subject-pictures. It well illustrates the quality of his imagination and his manner of painting in grey and brown hazes enriched with warmer colours. In a curious sense his pictures of this type, with their reminiscences of Delacroix (and of Rembrandt and the Venetians), bridge the gap between Romanticism and Impressionism. This canvas was in the famous Salon des Refusés of 1863, when the more progressive painters of the period who were rejected from the official Paris Salon held their own exhibition.

Oil on canvas, $38\frac{1}{2}'' \times 51\frac{1}{4}''$.

LITERATURE

Fantin-Latour, *Catalogue* (1911), p. 30, No. 214.
Gibson, *Fantin-Latour* (n.d.), pp. 48, 209.
Montreal Museum of Fine Arts, *Catalogue* (1960), p. 66.

EXHIBITED

Paris, Salon des Refusés, 1863, No. 158.
Paris, *Centennale de l'art français*, 1900.

Paris, *Fantin-Latour*, 1906, No. 142.
New York, *Fantin-Latour*, 1932.
London, Reid & Lefevre, 1934.
Ottawa, National Gallery, *French Painting*, 1934, No. 54.

EX COLLECTION

Charles-Édouard Haviland, Paris.
Acquired by the Montreal Museum through the Tempest Purchase Fund, 1936.

FRENCH SCHOOL

HENRI FANTIN-LATOUR 1836-1904

Portrait du jeune Fitz-James

THE ART GALLERY OF HAMILTON

Because of its simple composition, pure line, and straightforward expression, this small portrait of 1867 is one of Fantin-Latour's best. It is one of the paintings which were stolen from the Art Gallery of Hamilton in April 1960.

Oil on canvas, $20\frac{1}{2}'' \times 16\frac{3}{4}''$.

LITERATURE
Fantin-Latour, *Catalogue* (1911), p. 42, No. 301.
Canadian Art, xiii (1956), p. 243.

EXHIBITED
Paris, Salon of 1867.

Paris, *Fantin-Latour*, 1906, No. 33.
Toronto, Art Gallery, *Great Paintings*, 1940, No. 99.
Montreal, Museum, *Canada Collects*, 1960, No. 112.

EX COLLECTION
Albert Pra.
H. S. Southam, Ottawa.
Presented to the Art Gallery of Hamilton, 1948, by the
late H. S. Southam.

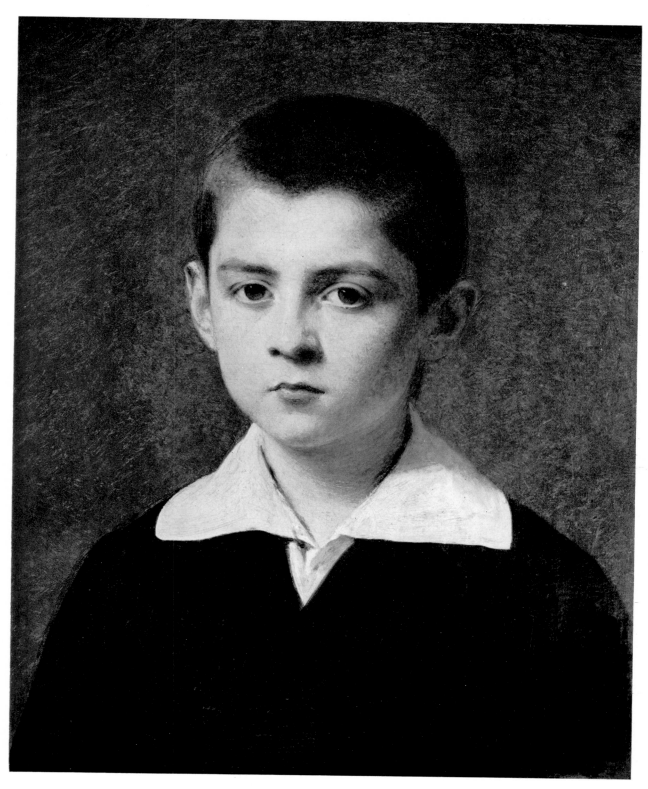

XII

XIII

HENRI FANTIN-LATOUR 1836-1904

Fleurs de cerisiers

COLLECTION OF MR AND MRS J. A. MACAULAY, WINNIPEG

This small study of cherry blossoms, painted in 1872, shows Fantin-Latour at his best in the handling of still life. This style is very different from that of the subject-pictures with their romantic hazes. Here, against a finely textured dark background, the transparent glass and the delicate white and green of the sprig of cherry stand out with glowing beauty. The simple composition and the exquisite treatment of the flowers combine to produce a picture of unity and great sensuous beauty. His art was a lovely blend of reticence and harmony.

Oil on canvas, $15\frac{3}{4}''\times 13''$.

LITERATURE

Fantin-Latour, *Catalogue* (1911), p. 71, No. 600.

EXHIBITED

Ottawa, National Gallery, *MacAulay Collection*, 1954, No. 51, reprod. in cat.

Winnipeg, Art Gallery, *Children and Flowers*, 1958, No. 28.

FRENCH SCHOOL

BERTHE MORISOT 1841–1895

Fillette à la poupée

COLLECTION OF MR AND MRS MAXWELL CUMMINGS, MONTREAL

Berthe Morisot was a granddaughter of the eighteenth-century master Fragonard. She and Mary Cassatt were the only two women to join the Impressionist circle. Fantin-Latour, whom she met in 1859, encouraged her to paint, as did Corot in 1860. In 1868 she married the younger brother of Édouard Manet. Early in her career she exhibited at the Salon, but later forswore it and participated in all but one of the Impressionist exhibitions. She had an important and continuing influence on Manet, persuading him to abandon his earlier manner (which involved the use of blacks) and to adopt the light-filled style of Monet, Pissarro, and Sisley. She appears as a model in some of Manet's pictures, and her letters are full of interesting and engaging comments about him. From about 1885 she was influenced by Renoir's style.

The artistic exchange between Berthe Morisot and Manet is illustrated in this charming study of a child. The interpretation of the child is personal and delightfully feminine. However, the objectivity of the scene and the simple composition are Manet's, and the freshness of colour and the flutter of the brushwork are in agreement with the style of the younger Impressionists. The picture was painted about 1883.

Oil on canvas, 28″ × 29″.

LITERATURE
Turner, *Canadian Art*, xvii (1960), p. 208, reprod.

EXHIBITED
Montreal, Museum, *Canada Collects*, 1960, No. 211.

EX COLLECTION
Mme Clément Rouart, Paris.

XIV

XV

FRENCH SCHOOL

EDGAR DEGAS 1834-1917

Danseuse rose

COLLECTION OF WILMOT L. MATTHEWS, OTTAWA

Degas was a leading Impressionist and one of the most distinctive painters of this period. He was born of a well-to-do family in Paris, where he lived all his life except for a trip to New Orleans and Spain in 1880. His father was a banker and his mother from New Orleans. In 1855 he was studying at the École des Beaux-Arts with Louis Lamothe (a pupil of Ingres) and Hippolyte Flandrin. At this time he met Fantin-Latour. From his academic training he derived a mastery of line that was to distinguish him from the majority of the Impressionists, who relied so much on the brush. At first his subjects were figures reflecting the influence of Ingres but later they were more concerned with everyday life. His seemingly casual compositions, which often comprised only a telling fragment of a scene, were partly inspired by Whistler and Manet in the sixties. Degas was in the first Impressionist exhibition in 1874, and about this time began his series of ballet dancers. In 1881 he began his series of sculptures. From about 1900 to his death he was almost blind.

The ballet gave Degas a subject-matter with a variety of angles of vision, unusual illuminations, and above all the opportunity to study the human figure in many poses. This picture, painted about 1878, is a relatively early one in the ballet series. At this time he was abandoning oils for the more flexible medium of pastel, which allowed him to capture a fleeting pose more easily and quickly, yet his pastels often have the strength and the depth of his oils. Here the characteristic pose of the dancer saluting the audience is brilliantly interpreted as a silhouette against a flat background. Despite his affection for the ballet he has painted this picture in a style that is essentially detached and unsentimental; it has a classic and everlasting quality.

Pastel on paper, 29½″ × 16½″.

LITERATURE
Lafond, *Degas,* ii (1919), reprod. following p. 36.
Studio, cv (1933), reprod. p. 228.
Lemoisne, *Degas,* ii (1946), p. 268, No. 487, reprod. p. 488.
Browse, *Degas Dancers* (n.d.), p. 390, reprod.

EXHIBITED
Paris, *Centennale de l'art français,* 1900, No. 878.
Paris, Galerie Petit, *Cent ans de peinture français,* 1930, No. 13.

Glasgow, *French Paintings,* 1930, 1934.
London, Tate Gallery, *French Paintings,* 1933.
Ottawa, National Gallery, *French Painting,* 1934, No. 43, reprod. in cat.
London, Reid & Lefevre, *French Masters,* 1937, No. 8.
Toronto, Art Gallery, *Loan Exhibition,* 1944, No. 17.

EX COLLECTION
Mme H. Laurent, Paris.
Mrs Wilmot Matthews, Toronto (1938-61).

EDGAR DEGAS 1834–1917

Chevaux de courses

THE NATIONAL GALLERY OF CANADA

Next to the ballet, race-horses were Degas's most famous subject-matter. This pastel is one of the finest examples, illustrating the means by which Degas realized his vision of contemporary life in flux. Strong colours play an important part here, but the main vehicle is the informal and animated design. The composition is a complex one in which the horses' legs are set to a quick rhythm that makes the whole scene come to life. The picture was painted between 1883 and 1885 and is closely related to another pastel which was once in the Jacques Seligmann Gallery (see Lemoisne No. 755).

Pastel on paper, 15″ × 22″.

LITERATURE
Vollard, *Album Degas* (1914), Pl. 8.
Lemoisne, *Degas*, iii (1946), p. 428, No. 756, reprod. p. 429; iv (1948), p. 114.
Canadian Art, viii (1950–1), p. 83; ix (1952), reprod. in colour, p. 138.
Fosca, *Degas* (1954), reprod. in colour, p. 82.

EXHIBITED
Paris, Galerie Weil, *Degas*, 1939, No. 40.
Ottawa, National Gallery, *Vollard Collection*, 1950, No. 10, reprod. in cat.

EX COLLECTION
Ambroise Vollard, Paris,
Acquired by the National Gallery of Canada, 1950.

XVI

XVII

EDGAR DEGAS 1834-1917

Au café-concert

COLLECTION OF MR AND MRS SAMUEL BRONFMAN, MONTREAL

Another characteristic Degas subject, a café interior, is represented in this oil, painted about 1884 in his middle period. It is a subject taken up by other painters, most notably Toulouse-Lautrec. With the diagonal of the woman's figure rising from the lower right almost to the top left, this is an example of Degas's daringly simple compositions. With its lovely iridescent colours, it also exemplifies his superb craftsmanship as a painter.

Oil on panel, 26″ × 19″.

LITERATURE
Vollard, *Album Degas* (1914), Pl. 71.
Hoppe, *Degas* (1922), p. 35, reprod.
Mauclair, *Degas* (1937), p. 65, reprod. in colour.
Lemoisne, *Degas*, iii (1946), p. 440, No. 773, reprod. p. 441.

EXHIBITED
San Francisco, Panama Pacific Exposition, 1915, *Department of Fine Arts*, No. 310.
Amsterdam, Stedelijk Museum, *Van Gogh and his Contemporaries*, 1930.
Toronto, Art Gallery, &c., *European Masters*, 1954, No. 61.
New York, Slatkin Galleries, *Renoir, Degas*, 1958, No. 1, reprod. in cat.
Montreal, Museum, *Canada Collects*, 1960, No. 178, reprod. in cat.

EX COLLECTION
Ambroise Vollard, Paris.
J. Strauss, Paris (sale, Dec. 1932, No. 35).
Girard, Paris.
Francis Salabert, Paris.

FRENCH SCHOOL

CAMILLE PISSARRO 1830-1903

Dulwich College

COLLECTION OF MR AND MRS J. A. MACAULAY, WINNIPEG

Pissarro, one of the leading French Impressionists, was born in St Thomas in the Virgin Islands of a Portuguese father and a West Indian mother. He worked in his father's shop until 1852, when he ran away to Venezuela with the Danish painter Fritz Melbye. He returned to St Thomas and was allowed by his family to go to Paris in 1855, arriving in time to see Courbet's paintings at the Exposition of 1855. Corot had an influence on him in his early period. He met Monet in 1859 and Cézanne in 1861. Between 1866 and 1869 he painted in the open air at Pontoise. In 1870 he fled the Franco–Prussian War and went to London, where he was influenced by the works of Constable. On his return he settled at Pontoise and went later to Louveciennes. In 1872 he introduced Cézanne to Impressionism and in 1874 participated in the first Impressionist exhibition. Like Monet, he was interested mainly in landscape and carried out most consistently of all the Impressionists the quasi-scientific investigation of light and colour in nature. He had an important influence on Gauguin, whom he met in 1877; he also met Seurat in 1885 and Van Gogh in 1886. He himself was influenced by Seurat's theories of the optical mixture of colours and technique of pointillism. He died in Paris.

Dulwich College is an early work of Pissarro, dating from his sojourn in England in 1871. It is painted in broad masses of colour and with fluid brushstrokes. These features, and the vibrancy of the light, show Constable's impact upon him at this time. The buildings represented in the picture are those of the College of God's Gift at Dulwich (now a part of London); they are a mixture of seventeenth-century and later elements.

Oil on canvas, $19\frac{3}{4}'' \times 23\frac{3}{4}''$.

LITERATURE

Pissarro and Venturi, *Pissarro* (1939), i, p. 95, No. 116; ii, Pl. 23.
Leymarie, *Impressionism*, i (1955), reprod. in colour p. 93.

EXHIBITED

London, Reid & Lefevre, *Renoir, Cézanne and their Contemporaries*, 1934, No. 24.

London, New Burlington Galleries, *Maîtres français*, 1936, No. 57.
Ottawa, National Gallery, *MacAulay Collection*, 1954, No. 16.

EX COLLECTION

Joseph Hessel, Paris.
F. Javal, Paris.
Sir David Eccles, London.

XVIII

CAMILLE PISSARRO 1830–1903

Rue à l'Hermitage, à Pontoise

THE NATIONAL GALLERY OF CANADA

This picture of 1875 is one of the best and most characteristic of Pissarro's early works. It comes from the period of relatively broad and simple painting, before he adopted the small touches of colour which are seen in his later phases. It was this style, with its large planes of composition, which influenced Cézanne at the outset of his career. The woman walking along the road is a reminder that Pissarro never completely scorned the human figure, in spite of his passion for the rendering of light and colour in the landscape. The picture was once catalogued by the National Gallery of Canada as *Ruelle à Auvers-sur-Oise*, but it has recently been identified by Dr Paul Gachet (the son of Van Gogh's doctor at Auvers) as the road leading to the Hermitage at Pontoise. It was one of the fine pictures which came to the National Gallery from the collection of the late Gordon C. Edwards of Ottawa.

Oil on canvas, 23″ × 36″.

LITERATURE

Pissarro and Venturi, *Pissarro* (1939), i, p. 123, No. 305; ii, Pl. 61.
Canadian Art, iii (1946), reprod. p. 124.
Art Quarterly, x (1947), p. 229, reprod. p. 230.
Hubbard, *National Gallery of Canada Catalogue*, ii 1959), p. 42, reprod.

EXHIBITED

Paris, Durand-Ruel, *Pissarro*, 1928, No. 21.
Amsterdam, Van Wisselingh & Co., *Peinture française*, 1929, No. 39, reprod. in cat.
Ottawa, National Gallery, *French Painting*, 1934, No. 84, reprod. in cat.
Montreal, Art Association, *19th Century Landscape Painting*, 1939, No. 90, reprod. in cat.
Paris, Orangerie, *Van Gogh et les peintres d'Auvers-sur-Oise*, 1954, No. 135.

EX COLLECTION

de Rochecouste.
Gordon C. Edwards, Ottawa.
Acquired by the National Gallery of Canada, 1946.

CAMILLE PISSARRO 1830-1903

Le Pont Boieledieu à Rouen, temps mouillé

THE ART GALLERY OF TORONTO

Towards the end of his life, when his health began to fail and he had stopped painting in the country, Pissarro undertook a series of townscapes which he observed from his hotel windows in Rouen. Painted in 1896, this much published and exhibited canvas is one of the best of the series of Rouen bridges. Its composition is dominated by the strong diagonal of the bridge, which recalls the unusual angles of vision seen in Japanese prints. Here one can see that Pissarro's style was less poetic but more robust than that of Monet and Sisley. He was always interested in the structure of a picture as well as in the fugitive effects of colour and atmosphere.

Oil on canvas, 29″ × 36″.

LITERATURE

Mauclair, *French Impressionists* (1903), reprod. p. 139.
Pica, *Impressionisti francesi* (1908), reprod.
L'Art français de la Révolution à nos jours (n.d.), reprod.
Les Arts, No. 147 (Mar. 1914), reprod.
Bulletin de la vie artistique (Feb. 1921), reprod.
Faure, *Histoire de l'art moderne* (1921), reprod.
Faure, *History of Art: Modern Art* (1924), reprod. p. 384.
Pissarro and Venturi, *Pissarro* (1939), i, p. 212, No. 948; ii, Pl. 191.
Art Gallery of Toronto, *Illustrations* (1959), reprod. p. 38.

EXHIBITED

Paris, Durand-Ruel, *Pissarro*, 1896, No. 4.

Paris, Durand-Ruel, *Pissarro*, 1910, No. 11.
Paris, Manzi & Joyant, *Pissarro*, 1914, No. 94.
Paris, Durand-Ruel, *Monet, Pissarro, Renoir, Sisley*, 1924, No. 38.
New York, Durand-Ruel, *Pissarro*, 1929.
Cleveland, Museum, *20th Anniversary*, 1936, No. 299.
Toronto, Art Gallery, *Trends in European Painting*, 1937, No. 35, reprod. in cat.
Toronto, Art Gallery, *Great Paintings*, 1940, No. 94.
Montreal, Art Association, *Masterpieces of Painting*, 1942, No. 60.
Pittsburgh, Carnegie Institute, 1958.
Presented by the Reuben Wells Leonard estate to the Art Gallery of Toronto, 1937.

XX

XXI

CLAUDE MONET 1840-1926

Les Rochers de Pourville

COLLECTION OF MR AND MRS LAZARUS PHILLIPS, MONTREAL

Monet was the real leader of Impressionism and remained the most faithful throughout his life to the principles of the movement. He was born in Paris but went as a child to Le Havre, where he met Boudin, who persuaded him to become a painter. He first saw the Japanese prints which had such an influence on his compositions about 1858. In 1859 he went to Paris and after his military service in Algeria he entered Gleyre's studio in 1862. Early in his career he met Pissarro, Whistler, and Manet, and in 1863 he painted with Renoir and Sisley at Barbizon. Jongkind and Courbet were among the painters who had an influence on him during his long career. He lived in England during the Franco-Prussian War and there he studied the works of Turner and Constable. On his return he experienced hard times, living on a house-boat while he painted on the Seine at Argenteuil. In 1874 he exhibited a painting called *Impression: soleil levant*, and from this he gained the epithet of Impressionist. Thereafter he exhibited with the others who came to be called Impressionists, including Pissarro, Renoir, Sisley, and Degas. Besides Argenteuil, he painted in Vétheuil and Belle-Île, the Italian Riviera, Antibes, and Giverny, where he spent the rest of his life after 1883 except for short trips to Holland, Norway, and Venice. About 1890 he began his famous series of poplars, water lilies, and haystacks, the Rouen Cathedral, and the Thames, all of which he painted many times at various seasons and times of day. In his last years his sight deteriorated and he had to be operated on for cataracts in 1920.

This fine seascape with the rocks of Pourville in the foreground was painted in 1882. It is remarkable not only for the fine impression it gives of the light and colour of a cloudy day at sea but for the use which Monet made of the separate brushstrokes to define the movement of the waves. Unlike the usual small touches of colour seen in his landscapes, these strokes form an almost rococo design on the surface of the canvas.

Oil on canvas, $25\frac{3}{4}'' \times 32''$.

EX COLLECTION
Ephrussi (1894).

Reinach de Camondo.
L. Reinach.
L. Becquart, Lille.
A. Dauré, Perpignan.

FRENCH SCHOOL

CLAUDE MONET 1840-1926

Vétheuil en été

THE ART GALLERY OF TORONTO

It was at Vétheuil, a village on the Seine, that Monet painted many of the finest and most characteristic works of his mature period. In this painting of 1879, his technique of colour division is seen to full advantage. Monet was like an eye—'but what an eye!', as Cézanne said—that received all the colour stimuli from his field of vision. He abolished local colour, observing that there were few solid areas of one colour in nature. Light, split up prismatically, was the only source of colour. In his paintings, the many small touches of pure colour were intended to blend with one another in the eye to produce a true image of the scene. The shadows which painters since the Renaissance had represented by adding greys or blacks to their colours were now represented by complementary colours placed together in close association. Space was indicated by a succession of colours into the distance and not by linear perspective. The fleeting effects of light and atmosphere which he captured were the great achievement of Impressionism. In their analysis of nature the Impressionists reflected the scientific spirit of the nineteenth century. Monet and his colleagues, for example, are known to have studied the optical researches of the physicist Helmholtz.

Oil on canvas, $26\frac{3}{4}'' \times 35\frac{5}{8}''$.

LITERATURE

Art Gallery of Toronto, *Illustrations* (1959), reprod. in colour, p. 29.

EXHIBITED

Toronto, Art Gallery, *French Painting*, 1933, No. 27.
Toronto, Art Gallery, *19th Century French Artists*, 1936, No. 33.

Toronto, Art Gallery, *Trends in European Painting*, 1937, No. 36, reprod. in cat.
Montreal, Art Association, *19th Century Landscape*, 1939, No. 84, reprod. in cat.
Toronto, Art Gallery, *Great Paintings*, 1940, No. 103.
Toronto, Art Gallery, *Old Masters*, 1950, No. 27.
Toronto, Art Gallery, &c., *European Masters*, 1954, No. 68, reprod. in cat.
Acquired by the Art Gallery of Toronto, 1929.

XXII

XXIII

CLAUDE MONET 1840-1926

Le jardin de l'artiste à Giverny

COLLECTION OF MR AND MRS OSKAR FEDERER, MONTREAL

This canvas, painted by Monet in 1881, has an unusual and striking effect. The simple massing of the composition into two balanced halves recalls the general influence which the Japanese print had on him in his early life. The hill-side garden offered him an area rich in colours and an opportunity to render space chromatically rather than by linear means. Human figures, such as the two children on the garden steps, are relatively rare in Monet's paintings.

Oil on canvas, $39\frac{1}{2}''\times 32''$.

LITERATURE
Malingue, *Monet* (1943), Pl. 113.
Turner, *Canadian Art*, xvii (1960), p. 205, reprod. p. 207.

EXHIBITED
Amsterdam, Stedelijk Museum, 1938-9 (loan).
Montreal, Museum, *Montreal Collections*, 1949, No. 41.
Montreal, Museum, *Canada Collects*, 1960, No. 159, reprod. in cat.

EX COLLECTION
Cassirer, Berlin.

CLAUDE MONET 1840-1926

Waterloo Bridge

COLLECTION OF HERMAN LEVY, O.B.E., HAMILTON

In 1903 Monet painted an exhaustive series of canvases of Waterloo Bridge in London, under changing conditions of light and atmosphere. The National Gallery of Canada has one of the same series and date, in which the bridge is almost swallowed up in the fog. In Mr Levy's picture the forms stand out more clearly and give the composition a greater firmness. The design shows a certain affinity to Whistler's nocturnes of the Thames, and like them it is a symphony in blues and greys.

Oil on canvas, 25½″ × 39¼″.

LITERATURE
Gaunt, *Observer's Book of Painting* (1958), Pl. 23.

EXHIBITED
Berlin, Galerien Thannhauser, *Monet*, 1928, No. 59, reprod. in cat.
London, Marlborough Gallery, 1958.

XXIX

XXX

FRENCH SCHOOL

ALFRED SISLEY 1839–1899

Les Côteaux de Bougival

THE NATIONAL GALLERY OF CANADA

Born in Paris of English stock, Alfred Sisley was sent to England in 1856 to begin a business career. The following year, however, he returned to Paris, and in 1862 entered the École des Beaux-Arts as a pupil of Gleyre, in company with Monet and Renoir. About 1865 he began painting landscapes in the open air at Fontainebleau. His family suffered financial loss and he had a difficult time for some years. He spent the period of the Franco-Prussian War in England, returning to paint in the region of Paris between 1872 and 1880. He exhibited with the Impressionists from their first exhibition in 1874. His landscapes are close in style to Monet, who influenced him greatly, especially after 1880. In 1883 he went to live at Moret-sur-Loing, where he died.

Les Côteaux de Bougival, a river scene on the Seine, is an early work of Sisley, painted in 1875. It shows a liquid handling of the pigment that was to disappear in his later, more drily painted canvases. His art was not as robust as that of Monet and Pissarro but was serene and tender, often with an undertone of melancholy.

Oil on canvas, 19¾″ × 23½″.

LITERATURE

Geffroy, *Sisley* (1935), Pl. 20.
Art Quarterly, xvi (1953), p. 352.
Daulte, *Sisley* (1959), No. 179, reprod.

EXHIBITED

Paris, Galerie Petit, *Sisley*, 1897, No. 145.
Amsterdam, Van Wisselingh & Co., *Peinture française*, 1929, No. 48, reprod. in cat.

Amsterdam, Van Wisselingh & Co., *Maîtres français*, 1952, No. 29, reprod. in cat.

EX COLLECTION

Feder, Paris (sale, Durand-Ruel, 25 June 1892).
Abbé Gauguin (sale, Hôtel Dupont, Paris, 6 May 1901, No. 18).
M. P. Voûte, Amsterdam.

FRENCH SCHOOL

PIERRE-AUGUSTE RENOIR 1841-1919

Tête de napolitaine

THE MONTREAL MUSEUM OF FINE ARTS

Renoir, the son of a tailor, was born at Limoges, but lived in Paris from the age of four. At thirteen Renoir started to paint porcelain, and in 1861 he entered Gleyre's studio at the École des Beaux-Arts, where Monet and Sisley were his fellow pupils. At this time he was influenced by Courbet and the eighteenth-century French painters. By 1866 he was painting landscapes at Fontainebleau. Later, he worked with Monet at Bougival, developing an Impressionist style, and participated in the first Impressionist exhibition in 1874. He made two trips to North Africa, and in 1881 he visited Italy, where his draughtsmanship became firmer. By 1883 he had developed a style quite different from that of the other Impressionists, for line and surface now began to play an important part in his work. His career was long, and he was a prolific painter, his later work being largely nudes and figure-pieces painted in hot colours. Rheumatism forced him to retire to the south of France in 1899, and, in his last years, to work with a brush strapped to his wrist. He died at Cagnes.

This exquisite head, painted in 1881, dates from Renoir's trip to Italy and is a record of the interest he then took in line and plastic form. As a small picture it affords a close view of his technique and reveals what a thoroughly sensuous painter he was. The painting of the flesh, with its delicate enamel-like tones and lovely iridescent colours, shows his understanding of and tender affection for his subjects. The picture was one of the first Renoirs to come to Canada, having been acquired by Sir William Van Horne in the early part of the century.

Oil on canvas, 14″ × 12″.

LITERATURE

Art News (4 Nov. 1933), p. 15, reprod.
Canadian Art, v (1948), reprod. p. 118.
Montreal Museum of Fine Arts, *Catalogue* (1960), p. 100.

EXHIBITED

Montreal, Art Association, *Van Horne Collection*, 1933, No. 146.
Montreal, Art Association, *Portraits*, 1941, No. 69.

Ottawa, National Gallery, *Art Association of Montreal Collection*, 1949.
Vancouver, Art Gallery, *French Impressionists*, 1953, No. 76.
Montreal, Museum, *Canada Collects*, 1960, No. 76.

EX COLLECTION

Sir William Van Horne, Montreal.
Bequest of Miss Adaline Van Horne to the Art Association of Montreal, 1945.

XXVI

XXVII

FRENCH SCHOOL

PIERRE-AUGUSTE RENOIR 1841-1919

Claude et Renée

THE NATIONAL GALLERY OF CANADA

As a work of Renoir from 1903, the *Claude et Renée* comes within his period of tender brushwork and iridescent colour that followed the 'Harsh Period' of 1884–90. It just precedes the ultimate period that was marked by a riot of colour. The painter's youngest son Claude is held by Renée, a servant who acted as model for many of Renoir's later paintings. The warm colours are muted and unified by the silvery tone which pervades the whole of this canvas. Until 1938 it belonged to another son, Jean Renoir.

Oil on canvas, 31″ × 25″.

LITERATURE

Vollard, *Renoir* (1925), reprod. opp. p. 154.
André, *Atelier Renoir* (1931), i, No. 284, Pl. 88.
Terrasse, *Cinquante portraits de Renoir* (1941), Pl. 37.
Canadian Art, vii (1950), reprod. p. 160.
Hubbard, *National Gallery of Canada Catalogue*, ii (1959), p. 45, reprod.

EXHIBITED

Paris, Bernheim Jeune, *Renoir portraitiste*, 1939 (hors catalogue).

Montreal, Watson Galleries, *French Artists*, 1948.
Vancouver, Art Gallery, *French Impressionists*, 1953, No. 79, reprod. in cat.
Toronto, Art Gallery, &c., *European Masters*, 1954, No. 74, reprod. in cat.
Los Angeles, County Museum, *Renoir*, 1955, No. 64, reprod in cat.

EX COLLECTION

Jean Renoir (until 1938).
Acquired by the National Gallery of Canada, 1949.

PAUL CÉZANNE 1839–1906

Paysage

COLLECTION OF MRS I. A. CHIPMAN, MONTREAL

Cézanne was the first and dominating influence on the art of the twentieth century. He was born and educated at Aix-en-Provence, where Émile Zola was his boyhood friend. His first drawing lessons were at the Musée Municipal at Aix. After studying law, briefly, in 1860–1, he went to Paris, where he met Pissarro and turned to painting. Delacroix, Daumier, Manet, and Courbet were among the early influences upon him. For a time he exhibited with the Impressionists, but after being rejected from the Salon he retired to Aix in 1879 and there worked in seclusion for the rest of his life. Out of Impressionism he created a style which was, in his own words, 'as solid and enduring as the art of the Galleries'. His work has been divided into six phases: (1) the Romantic Period from about 1860 to 1872; (2) the Impressionist Period from about 1872 to 1878, when he was under Pissarro's tutelage; (3) the Constructive Period from about 1878 to 1883; (4) the Further Development of the Constructive style from about 1883 to 1888; (5) the Period of Synthesis from about 1888 to 1896; and (6) the Last Years from 1896 to 1906.

This landscape, representing a scene near Aix-en-Provence, is an example of the style of the Constructive Period. It is dated by Lionello Venturi between 1879 and 1882. By this time he had abandoned his early Pissarro-dominated style and made the first great innovation of his career, the simplification of the landscape into a few strong elements. These he interpreted on canvas in terms of what he called 'cubes, spheres, and cones', assembling them all into a sturdy constructive design. This was the first step in the process which led to modern cubism and abstraction.

Oil on canvas, $17\frac{3}{4}'' \times 21\frac{1}{4}''$.

LITERATURE
Iavorskaia, *Cézanne* (1935), Pl. xii.
Venturi, *Cézanne* (1936), i, p. 132, No. 309; ii, Pl. 83.

EXHIBITED
London, Reid & Lefevre, 1935, No. 7.
Montreal, Scott & Son, *Renoir and his Contemporaries*, 1936, No. 18, reprod. in cat.
Montreal, Museum, *Montreal Collections*, 1949, No. 11.
Toronto, Art Gallery, &c., *European Masters*, 1954, No. 66.
Montreal, Museum, *Canada Collects*, 1960, No. 133, reprod. in cat.

EX COLLECTION
Ambroise Vollard, Paris.

XIXX

FRENCH SCHOOL

PAUL CÉZANNE 1839-1906

Prairie et ferme du Jas de Bouffan

THE NATIONAL GALLERY OF CANADA

Shown here are the chestnut trees at Le Jas de Bouffan, a country house near Aix which Cézanne's father bought in 1859. The picture was painted between 1885 and 1887 and thus comes within the period when he was elaborating upon the Constructive style. He had already discarded the fleeting effects of colour and light of his Impressionist Period in favour of his 'eternal' compositions and colour harmonies. But here, in contrast to the severe geometrical emphasis in pictures of the Constructive Period, he shows a new response to the charms of nature, as seen in the short brushstrokes, which are characteristic of this period. These brushstrokes superficially resemble the *touches* of the Impressionists but are really decorative in function. Yet in spite of this relaxation from the strictness of the preceding period, Cézanne still retained the constructive principle. He now used colour somewhat more than contour to indicate structure. Some critics regard the paintings of this date as the fullest realization of monumentality in his work. The picture was once owned by the German Impressionist Max Liebermann.

Oil on canvas, 26″ × 32½″.

LITERATURE
Blake, *Relation in Art* (1925), reprod. opp. p. 288.
Venturi, *Cézanne* (1936), i, p. 165, No. 466; ii, Pl. 140.
Hubbard, *National Gallery of Canada Catalogue*, ii (1959), p. 8, reprod.

EXHIBITED
New York, Rosenberg & Co., *Cézanne*, 1942, No. 8, reprod. in cat.
New York, Wildenstein & Co., *Cézanne*, 1947, No. 35.

EX COLLECTION
Max Liebermann, Berlin.
Dr Kurt Rietzler, New York.
Acquired by the National Gallery of Canada, 1954.

PAUL CÉZANNE 1839–1906

Portrait de paysan

THE NATIONAL GALLERY OF CANADA

The *Portrait de paysan*, one of a series of Cézanne's gardener at Aix, was painted about 1900 and is one of the finest works of his last period. The figure stands out impressively against the background of a plain wall. Its volume is fully realized in spite of the very limited colour scheme, mainly of blues and greys, and the forms are clearly defined by heavy dark outlines. Retaining the broad planes of his earlier periods, he has here arrived at a classic breadth of conception and a bravura in the technique of painting. The result is meaningful and powerful, and almost abstract in manner, the ultimate expression of a temperament in which force and discipline are nicely balanced.

Oil on canvas, $35\frac{3}{4}'' \times 29\frac{3}{4}''$.

LITERATURE
Venturi, *Cézanne* (1936), i, p. 218, No. 712; ii, Pl. 233.
Canadian Art, ix (1951–2), p. 74, reprod.
Hubbard, *National Gallery of Canada Catalogue*, ii (1959), p. 6, reprod.

EXHIBITED
Ottawa, National Gallery, *Vollard Collection*, 1950, No. 4, reprod. in cat.
Toronto, Canadian National Exhibition, 1952, No. 5.
Vancouver, Art Gallery, *French Impressionists*, 1953, No. 46.

Toronto, Art Gallery, &c., *European Masters*, 1954, No. 67, reprod. in cat.
The Hague, Gemeente Museum, *Cézanne*, 1956, No. 50, reprod. in cat.
Cologne, Wallraf-Richartz Museum, *Cézanne*, 1956, No. 80, reprod. in cat.
Zurich, Kunsthaus, *Cézanne*, 1956, No. 80, reprod. in cat.
Munich, Haus der Kunst, *Cézanne*, 1956, No. 62, reprod. in cat.

EX COLLECTION
Ambroise Vollard, Paris.
Acquired by the National Gallery of Canada, 1950.

XXX

XXXI

ODILON REDON 1840–1916

Vase de fleurs

THE ART GALLERY OF TORONTO

Redon was born at Bordeaux. His father was French and his mother came from New Orleans. He had his first art lessons in Bordeaux about 1855. Early in his life he turned for inspiration to the advanced literary men of his day, including Flaubert, Baudelaire, and Poe. He was also very fond of music. In 1857 he worked at architectural design in Bordeaux and then entered Gérôme's studio at the École des Beaux-Arts in Paris. Back in Bordeaux in 1863, he turned to graphic art and discovered the etchings of Rembrandt. He also tried art criticism. After the Franco-Prussian War he settled in Paris, where he worked with Corot and Courbet and was influenced by the religious painter Gustave Moreau. His work became known about 1880, and he was soon recognized as one of the leading symbolist painters. He painted two distinct types of pictures: the impressionistic flower-pieces and the symbolist fantasies. Writers such as Huysmans and Mallarmé and painters such as Maurice Denis were among his friends. He retired to his villa at Bièvres in 1909 and died in Paris.

This still life is a good example of Redon's impressionistic flower-pieces. The mixed flowers are rendered in a straightforward way but with an exquisitely personal touch. The picture was painted about 1915.

Oil on canvas, $25\frac{1}{2}'' \times 21\frac{1}{2}''$.

LITERATURE
Art Gallery of Toronto, *Illustrations* (1959), reprod. p. 57.

EXHIBITED
Toronto, Art Gallery, *Loan Exhibition*, 1935, No. 187.
Toronto, Art Gallery, *19th Century French Artists*, 1936, No. 35, reprod. in cat.
Toronto, Art Gallery, &c., *European Masters*, 1954, No. 71, reprod. in cat.
Acquired by the Art Gallery of Toronto, 1935.

PAUL GAUGUIN 1848-1903

Paysage à Pont-Aven

THE NATIONAL GALLERY OF CANADA

With Cézanne and Van Gogh, Gauguin was one of the principal Post-Impressionists. Born in Paris, he spent part of his childhood at Orléans, and after a few years at sea worked at the Paris banking house of Bertin. He began to draw about 1873, and later painted under the influence of Pissarro, whom he met in 1877. He exhibited with the Impressionists from 1881 to 1886. In 1883, after a crash in the financial world, he gave up his banking post and went to paint full-time with Pissarro. The next year he moved to Copenhagen, but he left his wife there and returned to Paris. In 1886 he went to live at Pont-Aven in Brittany, where he met Émile Bernard and became interested in medieval and primitive art. In October 1888 he visited Van Gogh at Arles, with disastrous results. The next year he exhibited paintings in his symbolist style with Bonnard and Maurice Denis. A trip to Panama and Martinique had given him a taste for the tropics, and in 1891 he left France for Tahiti. There he became sick and returned to Paris for a couple of years for lack of money. In 1901 he moved from Tahiti to the Marquesas Islands, where he died.

The Pont-Aven landscape in the National Gallery of Canada, painted between 1885 and 1887, antedates the symbolist phase of Gauguin's style. Instead it reflects the earlier influence of Pissarro and the divided colour of the Impressionists. But already a personal note is struck by the intensity of colour and the rather pronounced arabesques in the composition; these forecast the simplicity and power of his later style.

Oil on canvas, $23\frac{1}{2}'' \times 28\frac{1}{2}''$.

LITERATURE

Art Quarterly, x (1947), p. 231.
Canadian Art, v (1948), p. 201, reprod.
Hubbard, *National Gallery of Canada Catalogue*, ii (1959), p. 28, reprod.

EXHIBITED

Vancouver, Art Gallery, *French Impressionists*, 1953, No. 56, reprod. in cat.
Toronto, Art Gallery, &c., *European Masters*, 1954, No. 75.
London, Ontario, Art Museum, 1959.
Acquired by the National Gallery of Canada, 1947, with the help of a gift from the late H. S. Southam, Ottawa.

XXXII

XXXIII

FRENCH SCHOOL

VINCENT VAN GOGH 1853–1890

Tête de paysanne de Brabant

COLLECTION OF MR AND MRS J. A. MACAULAY, WINNIPEG

Vincent van Gogh, the most famous figure in late nineteenth-century painting, was the pioneer of Expressionism in modern art. Born at Groot Zundert in Holland, the son of a Protestant pastor, he tried several occupations, including those of art dealer (in The Hague, Brussels, London, and Paris) and evangelist, before turning to painting in 1880. He made drawings of the miners at Le Borinage in Belgium and worked in The Hague, where he met Anton Mauve. He painted at Nuenen in Brabant and in 1885 studied for a few months at the Antwerp Academy before going to Paris. In Paris he was influenced by the Impressionists, and met Toulouse-Lautrec and Gauguin. For a short time he adopted the pointillist technique of Seurat and Signac. During this period he was also influenced to some extent by the works of Rembrandt, Delacroix, Millet, Gustave Doré, and Monticelli. In February 1888, on the advice of Toulouse-Lautrec, he left Paris for Arles in Provence. In October he was visited by Gauguin, and in December, in mental turmoil, he cut off his ear and was put in hospital. His hallucinations continued until in May 1889 he entered the asylum at Saint-Rémy, where his violent crises were interspersed with lucid intervals. A year later he left to visit his brother in Paris, then went to Dr Gachet's hospital at Auvers-sur-Oise, where he died as a result of a revolver wound.

This study of the head of a peasant woman is a highly characteristic work of 1885, when Van Gogh was painting among the peasants at Nuenen. It is closely related to one of the main figures in the famous group *The Potato Eaters*. With their dark tones, emphatic brushwork, and strong characterization of the subjects, the pictures of this period show Van Gogh's seriousness of purpose and deep sympathy with his fellow human beings.

Oil on canvas, $15\frac{3}{4}'' \times 13\frac{1}{4}''$.

LITERATURE
De la Faille, *Van Gogh* (1928), i, p. 47, No. 141; ii, Pl. xl.
Moderne Kunstwerken, vi, No. 12, reprod.
De la Faille, *Van Gogh* (1939), p. 122, Pl. 139.

EXHIBITED
Amsterdam, Rijksmuseum, 1917–22 (loan).
Toronto, Laing Gallery, 1959.
Winnipeg, Art Gallery, *Winnipeg Collects*, 1960, No. 97, reprod. in cat.

EX COLLECTION
H. P. Bremmer, The Hague.

VINCENT VAN GOGH 1853-1890

Nature morte: fleurs

THE NATIONAL GALLERY OF CANADA

This is one of two Van Gogh flower-pieces in the collection of the National Gallery of Canada. It comes from the Paris period (1886-8) and reflects the general influence of the Impressionists. In particular, however, the flaky handling of the paint recalls the technique of the curious romantic painter Adolphe Monticelli, whose work had impressed Van Gogh. The inner agitation of his own temperament is of course already evident in the vigour of the brushwork. Every stroke seems to have an inner life of its own.

Oil on canvas, 19½″ × 24″.

LITERATURE

De la Faille, *Van Gogh* (1928), i, p. 74, No. 251; ii, Pl. lxvii.
De la Faille, *Van Gogh* (1939), Pl. 295.
Hubbard, *National Gallery of Canada Catalogue*, ii (1959), p. 30, reprod.

EXHIBITED

Amsterdam, Panorama, 1892.

Brussels, Palais des Beaux-Arts, *Van Gogh*, 1946, No. 54, reprod. in cat.
Venice, Biennale, 1948, *Impressionisti*, No. 90.
Toronto, Art Gallery, &c., *European Masters*, 1954, No. 76.
Vancouver, Art Gallery, 1957.
London, Ont., Art Museum, 1959.

EX COLLECTION

Oldenboom, Amsterdam.
Acquired by the National Gallery of Canada, 1951.

XXXIV

XXXV

VINCENT VAN GOGH 1853–1890

Iris

THE NATIONAL GALLERY OF CANADA

The growing frenzy of the last few months of Van Gogh's life is well illustrated in this picture of iris blooming in the fields near Arles. It was painted in 1888 or 1889. The agitated brushstrokes and the sharp-pointed swirling forms of the plants express a more intense emotional reaction to the power of natural growth than had ever been seen in the history of art. It is done very simply through the medium of pure colour. Here too is evidence of the speed at which he worked and of his desire to finish as many paintings as possible between spells of madness.

Oil on paper, $24\frac{1}{2}''\times 19''$.

LITERATURE

De la Faille, *Van Gogh* (1928), i, p. 169, No. 601; ii, Pl. clxvi.
Scherjon and De Gruyter, *Van Gogh* (1937), No. 183.
De la Faille, *Van Gogh* (1939), Pl. 591.
Canadian Art, xiii (1956), reprod. p. 252.
Hubbard, *National Gallery of Canada Catalogue*, ii (1959), p. 30, reprod.

EXHIBITED

Toronto, Laing Gallery, *French Painting*, 1953, reprod. in cat.
Winnipeg, Art Gallery, 1955.
Calgary, Jubilee Auditorium, 1957.
Vancouver, Art Gallery, 1957.

EX COLLECTION

J. H. Cosquino de Bussy, Amsterdam.
Wilhelmina van Gogh.
Acquired by the National Gallery of Canada, 1955.

FRENCH SCHOOL

ÉDOUARD VUILLARD 1868-1940

La Conversation

THE ART GALLERY OF TORONTO

Vuillard was born at Cuiseaux (Saône-et-Loire), the son of an army officer and a dress-maker. The family moved to Paris in 1877, where in 1886 he entered Gérôme's studio at the École des Beaux-Arts. Later he changed to the Académie Julian, where he met Maurice Denis, Bonnard, and Paul Sérusier. At this time he felt the influence of Gauguin and to some extent Toulouse-Lautrec and Japanese art. In 1889 he and his friends banded together as 'Les Nabis' and painted in a symbolist style. Vuillard's development of a personal style and his success as an artist date however from the nineties. Like Bonnard, he later became known for his intimate treatment of domestic subjects and of interiors in particular. Besides easel painting he made designs for the theatre and mural decorations for the Palais de Chaillot, the League of Nations, and other buildings. He is also known for his fine lithographs. He left Paris before the German advance in the Second World War and died at La Baule (Seine-Inférieure).

La Conversation was painted about 1893. It shows the sprightly figures, sparkling colours, and poetic intensity of expression that are characteristic of the Vuillard of this period when he was associated with the poet Mallarmé. Vuillard's interiors are probably the most successful modern conversation-pieces.

Oil on paper, 19¾″ × 24¾″.

LITERATURE
Canadian Art, v (1948), reprod. p. 166.
Ritchie, *Vuillard* (1954), reprod. p. 44.
Art Gallery of Toronto, *Illustrations* (1959), reprod. p. 58.

EXHIBITED
Boston, Institute of Modern Art, 1944.
New York, Museum of Modern Art, *Vuillard*, 1954.
Detroit, Institute of Arts, *Two Sides of the Medal*, 1954, No. 135.
Acquired by the Art Gallery of Toronto, 1937.

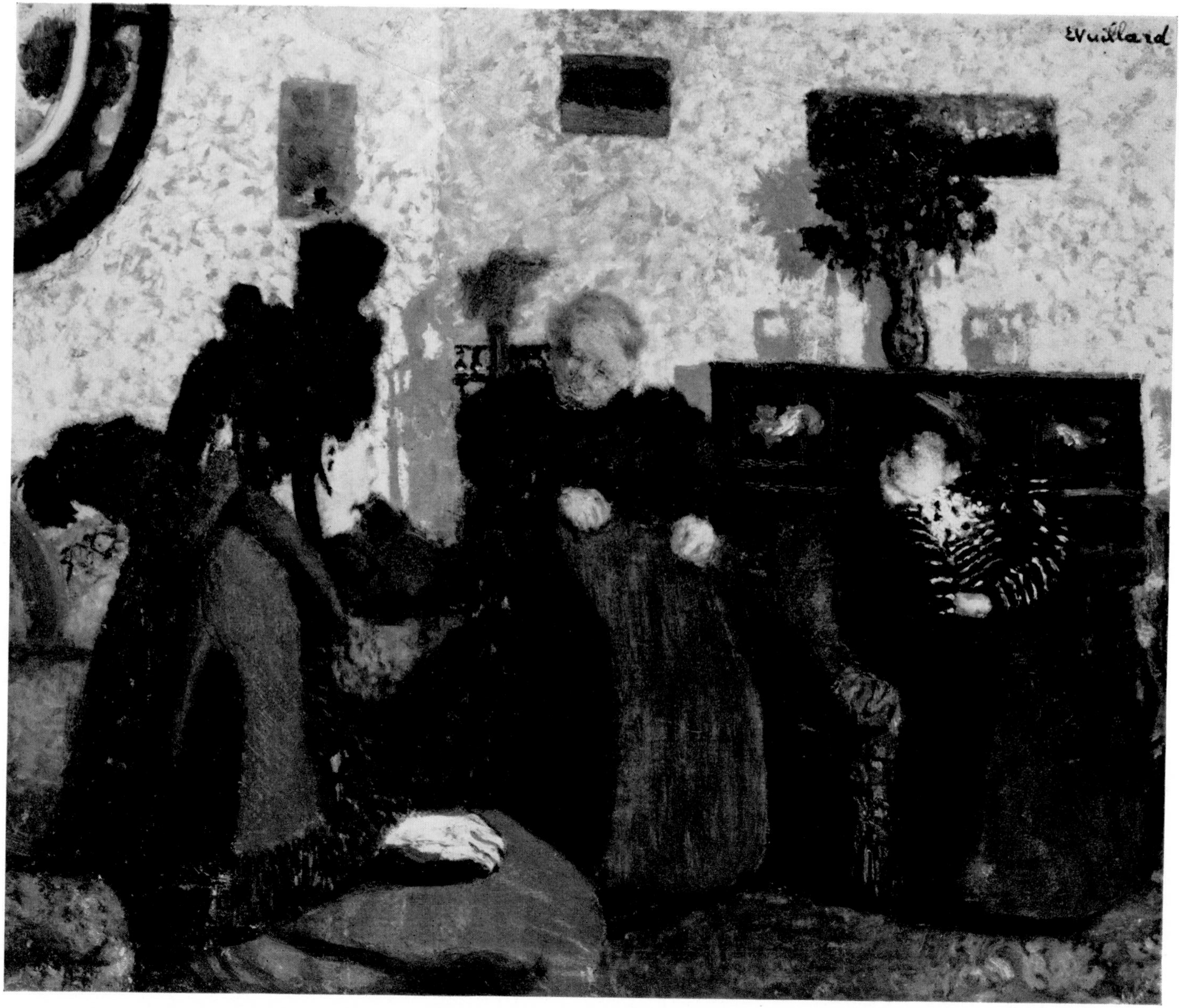

XXXVI

XXXVII

PIERRE BONNARD 1867-1947

La Table garnie

THE ART GALLERY OF TORONTO

Bonnard was born at Fontenay-au-Roses (Seine), the son of a government official. He studied law for a few years and then turned to painting. His first instruction was at the École des Beaux-Arts in 1888 and later at the Académie Julian, where he met Maurice Denis, Vuillard, and Paul Sérusier. The influence of Gauguin upon him at this time was decisive, but he was also influenced by Degas, Renoir, and Japanese art. He exhibited with the Nabis from 1891 to 1905, and then adopted the freer and more impressionistic style which became known as 'Intimisme'. In 1895 Ambroise Vollard published twelve of his lithographs. After 1900 he lived in and around Paris, and travelled quite extensively in Europe. He painted for a part of each year in the South of France and in 1925 bought a villa at Le Cannet, where he died.

This still life, painted about 1924, might be more correctly described as an interior. The homely objects on the table, informally grouped but carefully composed, are bound together by Bonnard's warm colours and enveloping atmosphere. Bonnard's careful draughtsmanship is apparent here; he once said, 'to represent on a flat surface masses and objects in space is a problem for the draughtsman'. Thus he did not rely solely on colour to indicate space as the Impressionists had done, and his work has a greater feeling of permanence.

Oil on canvas, 14½″ × 21½″.

LITERATURE
Studio, cxxxiv (1947), reprod. p. 55.
Art Gallery of Toronto, *Illustrations* (1959), reprod. p. 58.

EXHIBITED
Montreal, Watson Galleries, *Loan Exhibition*, 1935, No. 162.

Montreal, Art Association, *19th Century French Artists*, 1936, No. 21, reprod. in cat.
Toronto, Art Gallery, &c., *European Masters*, 1954, No. 78.

EX COLLECTION
Georges Bernard, Paris.
Acquired by the Art Gallery of Toronto, 1935.

PIERRE BONNARD 1867–1947

Le Port de Cannes

THE NATIONAL GALLERY OF CANADA

There is in Bonnard's work a romanticism that is somehow created of pure colours and flowing brushstrokes. His lyric and incandescent style is in the best tradition of French painting. This harbour scene is painted almost entirely in blues which are set off by small touches of warmer colours. While the colour is pervasive in its effect, the total impression is one of great subtlety. Equally satisfying is the composition of upright forms in the masts of the boats.

Oil on canvas, $16\frac{1}{2}'' \times 26''$.

LITERATURE
Canadian Art, ix (1952), p. 139.
Hubbard, *National Gallery of Canada Catalogue*, ii (1959), p. 1, reprod.

EXHIBITED
Amsterdam, Van Wisselingh & Co., *Maîtres français*, 1951, No. 3, reprod. in cat.
Toronto, Art Gallery, &c., *European Masters*, 1954, No. 77.

EX COLLECTION
Renaud, Paris.

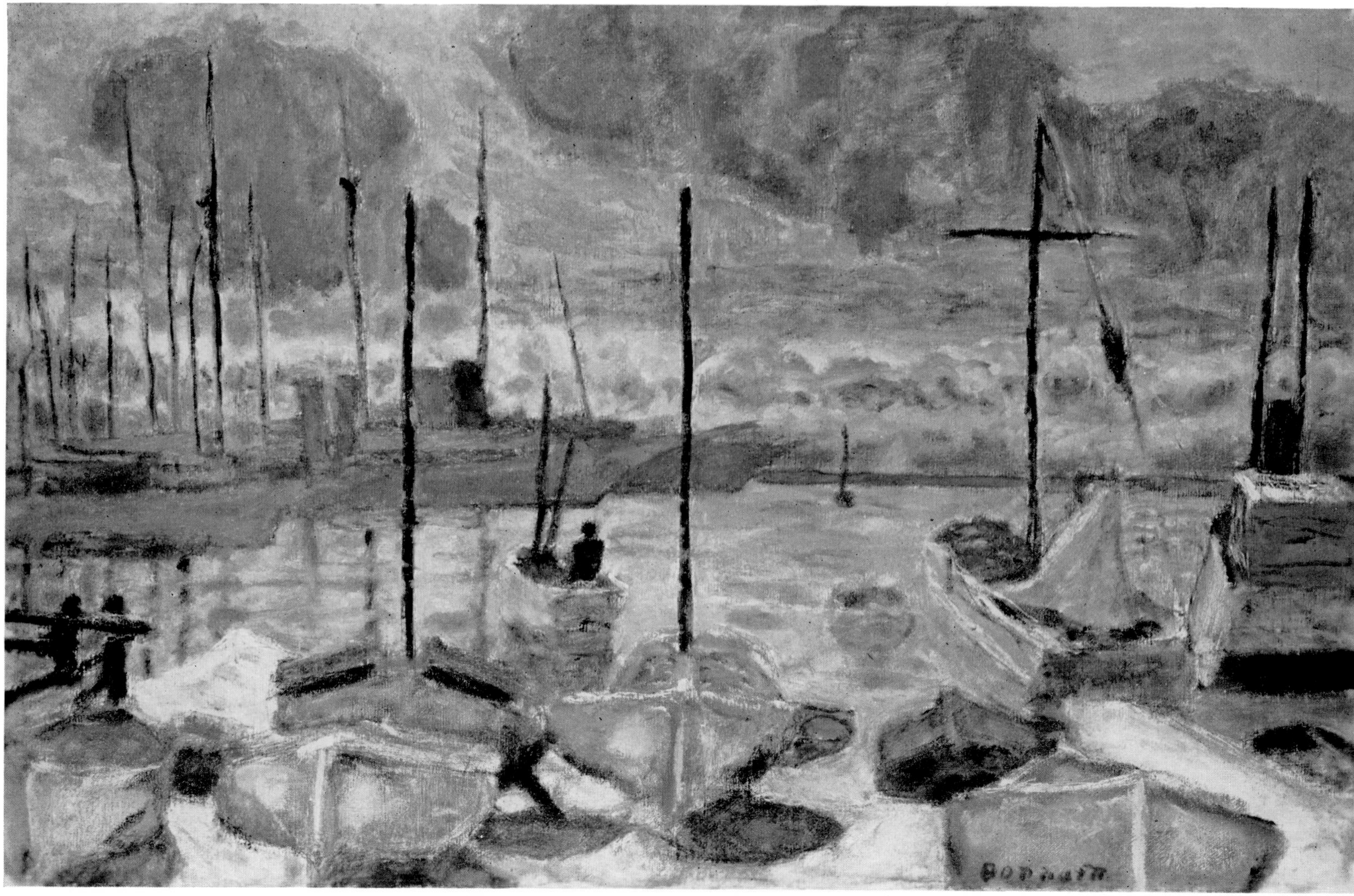

XXXVIII

XXXIX

GEORGES ROUAULT 1871-1958

Pierrette

COLLECTION OF DR AND MRS G. R. MCCALL, MONTREAL

Rouault was a highly individual figure who stood out sharply even among the many individual styles in modern painting. He was born in a Paris cellar during the bombardments of 1871. At fourteen he was apprenticed to a glass-painter engaged in the restoration of medieval windows, and this instilled in him a taste for deep glowing colours and heavy black lines. The leading exponent of religious art in the twentieth century, he began painting biblical subjects after his studies under Gustave Moreau at the École des Beaux-Arts. In 1898 he served briefly as curator of the Musée Moreau. In 1902 a meeting with the novelist Huysmans deepened his religious intentions in art, and his many representations of the Passion sounded an apocalyptic note in a materialistic age. At this time also he met Léon Bloy and began a series of subjects that expressed human misery. Though he exhibited with the Fauves in 1905 he did not continue with them for he had already gone further than they in designing in intense colours. Once he had formed his distinctive style he changed it little over the years. Besides painting, he designed for the ballet, made prints in an original mixture of media, and illustrated books by Baudelaire and others. In 1945 he was commissioned to design the glass in the church at Assy (Haute-Savoie). In 1948 he destroyed 315 of his paintings which had been returned to him from the Ambroise Vollard estate. He died in Paris.

Pierrette is one of Rouault's many studies of circus people, a class of beings which for him best personified the sadness of the human lot. The picture well illustrates his heavy impasto and strong black outlines; in it may be sensed the great interior force that underlay his art.

Oil on canvas, 30¼″ × 22¼″.

EXHIBITED

New York, Schoneman Galleries, *Rouault*, 1957, No. 17, reprod. in cat.

ALBERT MARQUET 1875-1947

L'Usine au bord du canal

COLLECTION OF HERMAN LEVY, O.B.E., HAMILTON

Marquet was born at Bordeaux. He went to Paris in 1895 and became a pupil of Gustave Moreau at the École des Beaux-Arts in company with Matisse and Rouault. By 1898 he had begun to paint landscapes in a manner which later developed into Fauvism. He began to exhibit in 1900, and from 1905 to 1908 he was one of the Fauves, sharing with them a preference for strong designs carried out in bright colours. Later he developed the gentler manner that is characteristic of his mature style. He travelled extensively, visiting Marseille, Rouen, Le Havre, Naples, Tangier, Venice, Rotterdam, and Hamburg; on one occasion he painted at Algiers with the Canadian painter James Wilson Morrice. In 1940 he left France for Algeria, where he lived for five years. He visited Russia in 1946 and died in Paris the following year.

L'Usine au bord du canal was painted in 1909 and thus dates immediately after the Fauve period. Though the colours are now more muted and grey than those of the Fauves, the simple flat design has been retained as a permanent feature of Marquet's style. Like Pissarro he used industrial subjects in his painting, recognizing them as an essential part of the modern scene.

Oil on canvas, $25\frac{1}{4}'' \times 31\frac{1}{4}''$.

EXHIBITED
Zurich, Kunsthaus, *Marquet,* 1948, No. 25.
Paris, Musée d'Art Moderne, *Marquet,* 1948, No. 16.

New York, Wildenstein, *Marquet,* 1953, No. 28, reprod. in cat.

EX COLLECTION
Viau.

FRENCH SCHOOL

MAURICE DE VLAMINCK 1876-1958

Les Écluses de Bougival

THE NATIONAL GALLERY OF CANADA

Vlaminck was a leading member of the group that included Matisse, Braque, Derain, Dufy, and others. Between 1905 and 1908 they made an important contribution to the development of modern painting by their creation of strong patterns of intense colours. This style earned for them the title of 'Les Fauves' (wild animals). Vlaminck was born in Paris, the son of a Belgian father and a mother from Lorraine, who were both musicians. He had his first art lessons in 1895, and also played the violin. In 1901 he wrote his first novel, which was illustrated by his friend André Derain, and, under the impact of Van Gogh and the Impressionists, turned definitely to painting. He participated in the Fauve exhibition of 1905 with Derain, Matisse, and Rouault. After 1908 he was influenced by Negro sculpture and by Picasso. In 1920 he moved to Auvers-sur-Oise and then to Reuil-la-Gadelière. By this time he had adopted the dark manner characteristic of his later period.

This landscape of 1908 with its vibrating reds and greens is eminently characteristic of the Fauve style. The influence of Van Gogh upon the Fauves is clearly seen in the strong design and emphatic brushwork.

Oil on canvas, $21\frac{3}{8}'' \times 25\frac{1}{2}''$.

LITERATURE
Sauvage, *Vlaminck* (1956), p. 111, Pl. 37.
Hubbard, *National Gallery of Canada Catalogue*, ii (1959), p. 50, reprod.

EXHIBITED
Montreal, Museum, *6 Centuries of Landscape*, 1952, No. 65, reprod. in cat.
Dallas, Museum for Contemporary Art, 1954.
Calgary, Jubilee Auditorium, 1957.
Acquired by the National Gallery of Canada, 1951.

FRENCH SCHOOL

RAOUL DUFY 1877–1953

Le Port du Havre

THE ART GALLERY OF TORONTO

Dufy was born at Le Havre, where in 1891 his family placed him with a firm of coffee importers. There he also had his first lessons in painting and met Othon Friesz, with whom he was later associated. In 1900 he was given a scholarship by the town of Le Havre to study at the École des Beaux-Arts in Paris. He was deeply influenced by the Impressionists and Cézanne and in 1901 saw the exhibition of Van Gogh's works, which also had an important effect on him. The paintings of Henri Matisse so influenced him that he became a member of the Fauves. By 1907, however, he had abandoned the strong Fauve colours and soon afterwards was attracted by the new trends in the work of Matisse and Picasso. He painted with Braque at L'Estaque in 1908. His later and more characteristic work, often carried out in water colours, was more linear and personal in quality. He travelled in Germany, England, Spain, North Africa, and the United States. He died at Forcalquier.

Le Port du Havre, which dates from 1905 or 1906, is one of Dufy's finest works of his early period; it is also a highly characteristic example of the Fauve style. The picture bears a dedication to Dr Maze, his physician at Le Havre.

Oil on canvas, $24'' \times 28\frac{3}{4}''$.

LITERATURE

Berr de Turique, *Dufy* (1930), p. 280, reprod. opp. p. 58.
Canadian Art, xi (1954), reprod. p. 70.
Art Gallery of Toronto, *Illustrations* (1959), reprod. p. 59.
Leymarie, *Fauvism* (1959), reprod. in colour p. 63.

EXHIBITED

San Francisco, Museum, *Dufy*, 1954, No. 3, reprod. in cat.

EX COLLECTION

Dr Maze, Le Havre.
Nancé, Le Havre.
Gift of the Women's Committee Fund to Com-
memorate the Golden Jubilee of the Art Gallery of
Toronto, 1953.

XLIII

ANDRÉ DERAIN 1880-1954

Tower Bridge, London

COLLECTION OF MR AND MRS J. A. MACAULAY, WINNIPEG

Derain was born at Chatou (Seine-et-Oise), the son of a baker, and started to paint when he was fourteen. While a pupil in Carrière's academy in Paris in 1898-9 he met Matisse and at about the same time met Vlaminck at Chatou. He also studied at the Académie Julian. Early in his career he was influenced by Van Gogh, whose works he saw at an exhibition in 1901, by Cézanne, and by Matisse, with whom he painted in the South of France. As one of the Fauves he exhibited with Matisse, Vlaminck, Rouault, and others. In 1910 he visited Spain, where he met Picasso and began to paint still life. By 1912 he was a Cubist and had developed what has been called his 'Gothic' manner. At this time also he felt the influence of Negro sculpture. His Cubist period ended after a couple of years, when he changed to a more naturalistic style. He is also known for his woodcuts, sculpture, and designs for the ballet.

Tower Bridge, London, is one of the most characteristic works of Derain's early period. It was painted on a visit to England in 1906 and illustrates the Fauve preference for strong compositions and bright colours. He and Vlaminck used the most brilliant colours of all the Fauves.

Oil on canvas, 26¼" × 39½".

LITERATURE

Haftmann, *Malerei im 20. Jahrhunderten* (1955), p. 66, reprod. in colour, Pl. 9.
Hilaire, *Derain* (1959), Pl. 25.
Dr Fritz Nathan und Dr Peter Nathan 25 Jahre 1936–1961 (1961), reprod. in colour, Pl. 54.

EXHIBITED

Cassel, Museum, *Dokumenta*, 1958.

EX COLLECTION

Emil Bührle, Zurich.

FRENCH SCHOOL

HENRI MATISSE 1869–1954

Femme à la fenêtre au bord de la mer

THE MONTREAL MUSEUM OF FINE ARTS

Matisse and Picasso were leaders of the School of Paris, which has had an important influence on painting all over the world. Matisse was born at Le Cateau-Cambrésis (Nord). In 1891 he went to study law in Paris, but he turned to painting and had his first lesson at the Académie Julian. The following year he became a pupil of Gustave Moreau at the École des Arts Décoratifs, where he met Albert Marquet. In 1895 he was at the École des Beaux-Arts in company with Rouault and in 1899 at Carrière's academy with Derain. In 1896 and 1897 he painted in Brittany and at this point was influenced by the Impressionists and Post-Impressionists. His first one-man exhibition was held in 1904. In 1905 he became a leader of the Fauve movement but by 1906 was already being influenced by Oriental art and was modifying his style. In 1910 he visited an exhibition of Islamic art in Munich with Marquet. His other travels included visits to Moscow in 1911 and North Africa where he painted with the Canadian James Wilson Morrice. Later he travelled to the South Seas and the United States. In 1938 he moved to Nice and in 1943 to Vence where in 1948 he devoted himself to the decoration of the Chapel of the Rosary. He died at Nice.

In 1921, at Nice, Matisse painted some of his finest figure compositions. These included several of the famous Odalisques in which he combined the figure with Moorish screens or carpets to form richly decorative designs. The following year a revived interest in landscape led him to clarify his perspective and to create much simpler compositions. In this canvas of 1922 the landscape is introduced very prominently. The perspective is anchored at the left by the vertical of the window. But the impression of space in his pictures never actually depends on linear perspective; it is achieved through an arrangement of the strokes of paint in such a way as only to suggest recession.

Oil on canvas, $28\frac{1}{2}'' \times 36\frac{1}{2}''$.

LITERATURE
Barr, *Matisse* (1951), p. 556.
Montreal Museum of Fine Arts, *Catalogue* (1960), p. 89.
Durand-Ruel, *Selection of Paintings* (1948), Pl. xv.

EXHIBITED
Montreal, Museum, *Manet to Matisse*, 1949, No. 20, reprod. in cat.
London, Ontario, Art Museum, 1959.

EX COLLECTION
Stephen C. Clark, New York.

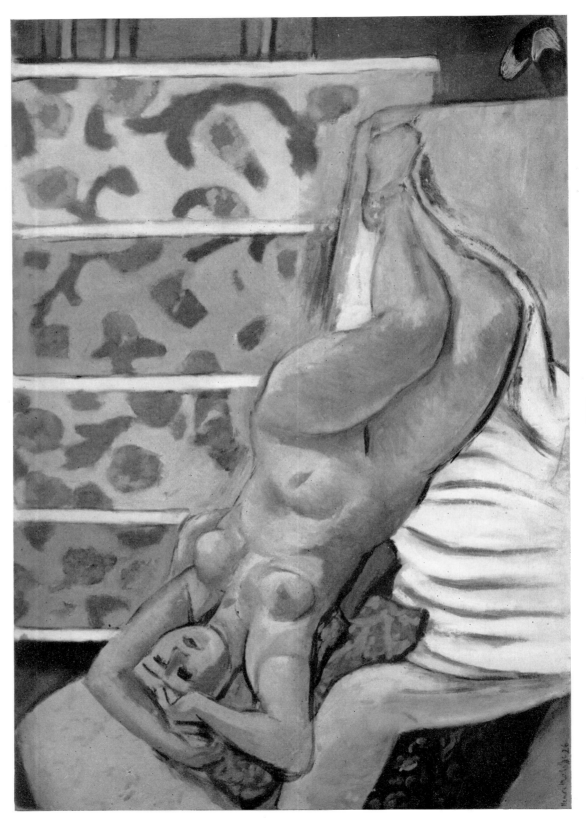

XLIV

HENRI MATISSE 1869-1954

Nu au canapé jaune

THE NATIONAL GALLERY OF CANADA

This picture enjoys the distinction of having been designated by the artist himself, shortly before his death, for the collection of the National Gallery of Canada. Painted in 1926, it represents the middle period of his development when he was under the influence of the draughtsmanship and colour values of Delacroix—a painter who had also come under the spell of the East a hundred years earlier. Thus Matisse intensified his colour and created the brilliant yet satisfying harmonies which are so well exemplified here in the lovely rose and blue of the flowered screen and the yellow of the drapery. Though the figure is firmly delineated, the space within the picture is indicated only by a succession of planes of colour.

Oil on canvas, $21\frac{1}{4}'' \times 32''$.

LITERATURE

Matisse (n.d.), reprod. in colour, Pl. vii.
Aragon, *Apologie du luxe* (1946), vi (Matisse), reprod. in colour.
Buchanan, *Canadian Art*, vii (1950–1), p. 64, reprod. p. 65.
Hubbard, *National Gallery of Canada Catalogue*, ii (1959), p. 203, reprod.

EXHIBITED

Berlin and Lucerne, Galerie Thannhauser, *Matisse*, 1930, No. 65.
Philadelphia, Museum, 1940.
Lucerne, Kunstmuseum, 1949.
Nice, Galerie des Ponchettes, *Matisse*, 1950, No. 25.
Venice, Biennale, 1950, *France*, No. 34.
Paris, Salon d'Automne, 1955.
Paris, Musée d'Art Moderne, *Matisse*, 1956, No. 73.

EX COLLECTION

Henri Matisse estate, Paris (1954–8).
Acquired by the National Gallery of Canada, 1958.

GEORGES BRAQUE 1882–

Le Port d'Anvers

THE NATIONAL GALLERY OF CANADA

One of the major figures in twentieth-century painting, Braque was born at Argenteuil (Seine-et-Oise). When he was eight his family moved to Le Havre and at seventeen he was apprenticed to his father, a house-painter. In 1900 he went to Paris and in 1902 entered the École des Beaux-Arts, after which he transferred to the Académie Humbert. He met Dufy in 1904 and exhibited with him and the other Fauves in 1906. In 1907 he met Picasso and Guillaume Apollinaire, and under the influence of Cézanne's works he turned to cubism. For a time his style was close to that of Picasso in the latter's periods of Analytical Cubism and Synthetic Cubism. By 1920, however, he had abandoned cubism for the freer and more personal style of his mature period. He has made designs for the ballet and painted a number of mural decorations.

Le Port d'Anvers was painted in the early summer of 1906 when Braque visited Antwerp with Othon Friesz and took rooms in a pension overlooking the harbour. Each artist painted a picture of the scene from the balcony. That of Friesz is in the collection of Robert Lebel, Paris. Braque's version in the National Gallery of Canada is one of the most important Fauve paintings and has been in a number of exhibitions.

Oil on canvas, 19⅝″ × 24″.

LITERATURE
Leymarie, *Fauvism* (1959), p. 106, reprod. in colour, p. 105.
Russell, *Braque* (1959), Pl. 2.
Hubbard, *National Gallery of Canada Catalogue*, ii (1959), p. 3, reprod.

EXHIBITED
Basle, Kunsthalle, *Braque*, 1933, No. 1.
New York, Museum of Modern Art, &c., *Les Fauves*, 1953, No. 14, reprod. in cat.
Buffalo, Albright Art Gallery, 1955.
Winnipeg, Art Gallery, 1955.
Edinburgh, Festival, 1956, *Braque*, No. 4, reprod. in cat.
Brussels, Exposition Internationale, 1958, *50 ans d'art moderne*, No. 36, reprod. in cat.
Acquired by the National Gallery of Canada, 1951.

XLVII

GEORGES BRAQUE 1882-

Vase gris et palette

COLLECTION OF MR AND MRS JOHN DAVID EATON, TORONTO

The 'Decorative Period' in Braque's development, which he entered in 1933, is well illustrated in this picture of 1938. At this time his style was characterized by warm colours, including pinks, by rich and varied surface textures, and by a delicate and ornamental play of line. Only faint reminiscences are left of the earlier Cubist phase, while a free design on a flat surface and a chord of browns, pinks, and greys play the leading roles in this picture.

Oil on canvas, 42″ × 35″.

EXHIBITED
Toronto, Art Gallery, *Loans*, 1959.
Montreal, Museum, *Canada Collects*, 1960, No. 197.

PABLO PICASSO 1881-

Femme assise

COLLECTION OF MR AND MRS G. HAMILTON SOUTHAM, OTTAWA

Picasso, the great individual genius of twentieth-century painting, sums up in his own development all the stylistic currents of the past fifty years. The many periods of his style succeed one another with astonishing rapidity. He was born at Málaga, where his father was an art teacher. He entered the Barcelona Academy in 1895 and the Madrid Academy in 1897, but soon set himself up as an independent artist. When he began his Blue Period (1900–4) he visited back and forth in Paris, and finally settled there in 1904. Then he met Guillaume Apollinaire and Gertrude Stein and began his Rose Period (1905–6), during which he was influenced by Egyptian art. Later he met Matisse, Derain, and Braque and began his Negro Period (1907–8). In 1908 he worked on the basis of Cézanne's style towards a geometric analysis of all objects in a scene and thus began his period of Analytical Cubism (1909–12). This was followed by his periods of Pasted Paper and Relief (1912–14) and of Synthetic Cubism (1912–19). In 1920 he started his Classical Period, but by 1923 he was painting in a Classic and a Surrealist style at the same time. Between 1929 and 1931 he painted sculptural forms. In 1934 he went to Spain and championed the Republican cause; the result is seen in the famous mural *Guernica*. He remained in France during the Occupation and since the war has continued to develop his style, including in his work sculpture and ceramics as well as painting.

Femme assise was painted about 1903, during the Blue Period. With its pathos of expression it shows the effect which El Greco and other Spanish Renaissance painters had on him. It also reflects the strong sympathies he had with the poor in Spain; and this brooding over the human condition was to remain with him for the rest of his life.

Oil on canvas, 32″ × 21¼″.

EXHIBITED
Ottawa, National Gallery, *Vollard Collection*, 1950, No. 15, reprod. in cat.

Ottawa, National Gallery, *Paintings in Ottawa Collections*, 1959.

EX COLLECTION
Ambroise Vollard, Paris.

XLVIII

XLIX

FRENCH SCHOOL

PABLO PICASSO 1881-

Le Guéridon

This canvas of 1919 comes from the end of Picasso's period of Synthetic Cubism. It was painted at Saint-Raphaël during a holiday on the Riviera, and is one of a series of pictures in various media of a subject Picasso used in different ways until 1925. A small table is piled high with fragments of still life, and the whole tends to merge with the wainscot and wallpaper of the room and with the sea and sky outside the window. The separate forms of the table and still life have been taken apart and reassembled into an exciting design of angular and clashing forms that may be described as the equivalent in painting of jazz in music. Yet the colours form a quiet harmony of blues, browns, and roses. A closely related painting, also of 1919, is in the Smith College Museum at Northampton, Massachusetts.

Oil on canvas, $45\frac{3}{4}'' \times 28\frac{3}{4}''$.

LITERATURE
Raynal, *Picasso* (1953), reprod. in colour, p. 71.
Zervos, *Picasso*, vi (1954), No. 1356, reprod.
Boeck, *Picasso* (1955), reprod.
Elgar and Maillard, *Picasso* (1956), reprod. (under 1919).
Art Quarterly, xx (1957), p. 479, reprod. p. 476.
Canadian Art, xv (1958), reprod. in colour, p. 25.

EXHIBITED
Milan, *Picasso*, 1953, No. 3, reprod. in cat.
Paris, *Picasso*, 1955, No. 48, reprod. in cat.
Munich, Haus der Kunst, &c., *Picasso*, 1955, No. 42, reprod. in cat.
Acquired by the National Gallery of Canada, 1957.

FERNAND LÉGER 1881–1955

Nature morte

COLLECTION OF MR AND MRS SAMUEL ZACKS, TORONTO

Léger was one of the leading figures in the development of Cubism in modern painting. He was born at Argentan in Normandy. At first he was apprenticed to an architect at Caen but by 1900 was in Paris working as a draughtsman. In 1903 and 1904 he studied painting at the École des Beaux-Arts and the Académie Julian. He was early influenced by the Impressionists and Neo-Impressionists and by Cézanne and Matisse. He met Picasso and Braque in 1910 and began to develop his own style, which involved the use of geometric and dynamic forms that suggested machinery and architecture. In 1920 he met Le Corbusier who was interested in machine design as well as in architecture and painting. Léger also painted compositions of massive figures with robot-like forms. In the twenties he designed for the ballet and made the first abstract film. He spent the Second World War in New York, with visits to Montreal. He died at Gif-sur-Yette.

This still life, painted in 1919, illustrates the pipe, piston, and cog forms found in Léger's work of the Cubist period. The brilliant colours have a metallic sheen. But the picture is no mere design for machinery; it amounts to an intellectual summing-up and poetic interpretation of modern mechanized civilization.

Oil on canvas, 47″ × 34½″.

EXHIBITED
Toronto, Art Gallery, &c., *Zacks Collection*, 1956, No. 55, reprod. in colour in cat.

L

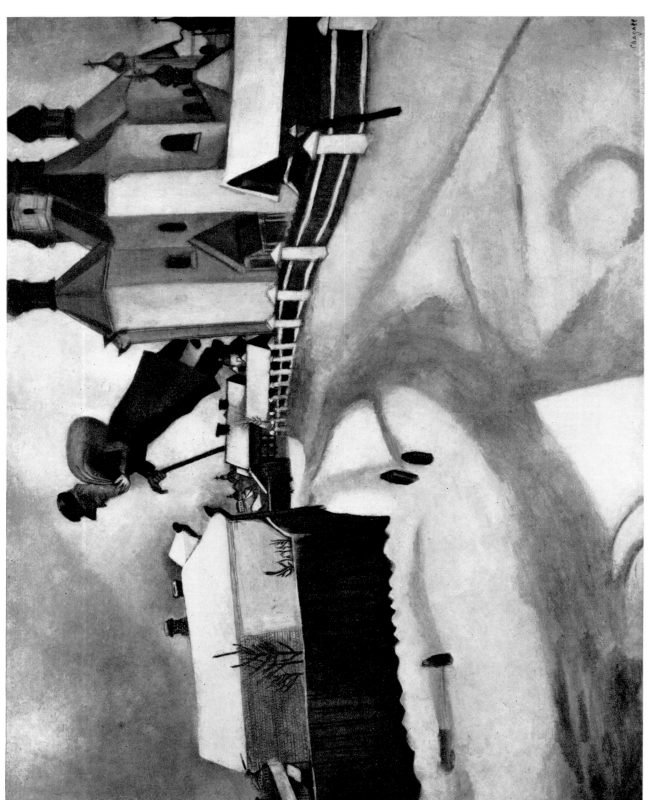

FRENCH SCHOOL

MARC CHAGALL 1887-

Au-dessus de Vitebsk

COLLECTION OF MR AND MRS SAMUEL ZACKS, TORONTO

Chagall was born at Liozno, near Vitebsk, in a strongly Jewish district of White Russia. He had his first lessons at Vitebsk and in 1907 went to St Petersburg Academy. In 1910 he was in Paris, where he met Guillaume Apollinaire, Modigliani, and the Cubist painter Robert Delaunay. From 1912 he exhibited at the Salon des Indépendants. He returned to Russia in 1914 and after the Revolution founded a progressive art school at Vitebsk and made theatre designs in Moscow. He left Russia in 1922, went first to Berlin, and then settled in Paris. He had now formed his characteristic style, in which he combined Jewish and Russian folklore with his own free fantasy. By 1930 he had become concerned with the growth of totalitarianism and was developing his art along social and religious lines. He fled France in 1941 and lived in the United States until 1947, when he returned to France. He is the illustrator of various books, including the *Fables* of La Fontaine and Gogol's *Dead Souls*.

Au-dessus de Vitebsk is an important early painting of Chagall's, dating from 1914 when he was living in Russia. It is highly characteristic of his personal type of expression. Here he presents a vision of his own town in winter, with the snow finely painted in tones of blue and violet. All is still, cold, and peaceful except for the portentous figure of the descending Jew. This subject was a persistent dream of Chagall's, perhaps induced by the pogroms that took place in Russia in the early part of the century.

Oil on paper, 27½″ × 35¼″.

LITERATURE
Venturi, *Chagall* (1956), reprod. in colour, p. 48.

EXHIBITED
Toronto, Art Gallery, &c., *Zacks Collection*, 1956, No. 11, reprod. in cat.

FRENCH SCHOOL

MAURICE UTRILLO 1883-1955

La Maison de Berlioz et Pavillon de chasse Henri IV

THE ART GALLERY OF TORONTO

Maurice Utrillo was the son of Suzanne Valadon, who had sat as a model for Renoir, Degas, and Toulouse-Lautrec, and was a painter in her own right. He was adopted in 1891 by Miguel Utrillo, a Spanish art critic. From 1905 he always added the *V.* of his mother's name to his signature. He became a drunkard and drug addict as early as 1901 and spent much of his time after that in hospitals. His mother made him paint in order to distract his attention. His paintings were mostly views of towns, their compositions often based on postcard views. His style changed relatively little throughout his life, though an Impressionist Period may be distinguished between 1902 and 1905, a White Period between 1908 and 1910, and a Multicolour Period in 1927. His works show a fine feeling for large planes, sensitive tonalities, and precise drawing as well as a nostalgic expression of the scenes themselves.

This picture was painted about 1909 during the White Period, the productions of which are the most highly prized by collectors. Besides the general qualities already noted it exhibits a calm and muted symphony of colours in the leaden sky, white walls, and red roofs. This and the complex pattern of the composition, with its interlace of bare branches, makes it one of Utrillo's most important early works. The scene is in Montmartre. The house in the lower left corner was occupied by Berlioz from 1834 to 1837. The house at centre is presumably that which Utrillo understood to be the hunting lodge of Henri IV. There was a tradition that it stood in the vicinity, but both houses have since been removed and the area covered with large modern buildings.

Oil on canvas, $21\frac{1}{4}"\times 28\frac{3}{4}"$.

LITERATURE

Werner, *Utrillo* (1955), reprod. in colour, Pl. 24.
Art Gallery of Toronto, *Illustrations* (1959), reprod. p. 59.
Pétridès, *Utrillo*, i (1959), No. 120, reprod.

EXHIBITED

Paris, Galerie André Schoeller, *Utrillo*, 1934, No. 30.
London, Tooth & Son., *La Flèche d'or*, 1935, No. 29.

Toronto, Art Gallery, *19th Century French Artists*, 1936, No. 38.
Montreal, Art Association, *6 Centuries of Landscape*, 1939, No. 68, reprod. in cat.

EX COLLECTION

G. Coquiot, Paris.
Pierre Faure, Paris.
Acquired by the Art Gallery of Toronto, 1935.

ITALIAN SCHOOL

GINO SEVERINI 1883–

Abstract Rhythm of Madame S.

COLLECTION OF MR AND MRS SAMUEL ZACKS, TORONTO

Severini, one of the leaders of the Futurist movement in Italian painting, was born at Cortona. In 1901 he met Boccioni, who was to become the theoretician of Futurism, and in 1902 Giacomo Balla, who was his first teacher. In 1906 he moved to Paris, where he was influenced by Seurat's pointillist technique and made friends with Picasso and Guillaume Apollinaire. In 1909 he signed the Futurist manifesto with Boccioni, Marinetti, and Carlo Carrà. The group held its first exhibition in 1912. Severini was at this time deeply affected by the French Cubists and relayed their influence to his fellow-painters in Italy. By 1921, however, he was painting in a neo-classical manner. He has made mural decorations in fresco and mosaic for several churches at Fribourg, Lausanne, and elsewhere in Switzerland.

This picture represents the early and Futurist phase of Severini's work. It was painted in 1912 at the height of the movement and well illustrates the impression which Cubism made upon him. The forms of the young woman and her dog have been broken up into many small facets and reassembled into a flashing, angular design of light and dark shapes. The total effect is rather different from that of a picture by Picasso or Braque, for here the analysis is noticeably less stringent and the design more decorative and amusing.

Oil on canvas, $36\frac{1}{4}''\times 25\frac{1}{2}''$.

EXHIBITED

Toronto, Art Gallery, &c., *Zacks Collection*, 1956, No. 105, reprod. in cat.

Montreal, Museum, *Canada Collects*, 1960, No. 195, reprod. in cat.

LIII

LIV

ITALIAN SCHOOL

AMEDEO MODIGLIANI 1884–1920

Beatrice Hastings in a Wicker Chair

COLLECTION OF MR AND MRS SAMUEL ZACKS, TORONTO

Modigliani was born at Leghorn, the son of a banker who belonged to an old Italian-Jewish family. He had his first lessons at Leghorn in 1898 but in the same year he contracted tuberculosis. By 1902 he was studying at the Florence Academy and in 1903 he was in Venice. His early style was moulded by the Italian tradition of line and sculptural form. Though he went to Paris (in 1905 or 1906) and painted there for the rest of his life, he is considered by many to be the best representative Italian painter of the modern period and not really French. He first exhibited in Paris in 1908. In his earliest works he showed the influence of Toulouse-Lautrec, but by 1910 he had developed his characteristic style based on African sculpture, and the works of Cézanne and Picasso. His short life was turbulent. He was addicted to drink and drugs and died of tuberculosis in Paris at the age of thirty-six.

Beatrice Hastings was an English poetess whom Modigliani met through his friend Ossip Zadkine. He had a love affair with her in 1914 but she could not curb his wild excesses. This picture of her, with its fine design in the flat and its firm structure of line, might be described as a continuation of the tradition of Botticelli into the twentieth century. It was painted in 1915.

Oil on board, 22″ × 18¼″.

LITERATURE
Roy, *Modigliani* (1958), reprod. in colour, p. 57.
Ceroni, *Modigliani* (1958), Pl. 35.

EXHIBITED
New York, Fine Arts Associates, *Modigliani*, 1954.
Toronto, Art Gallery, &c., *Zacks Collection*, 1956, No. 77, reprod. in cat.

Chicago, Arts Club, *Modigliani*, 1959.
Cincinnati, Art Museum, *Modigliani*, 1959, No. 5.

EX COLLECTION
Paul Guillaume, Paris.
Mme Jean Walter, Paris.
Henry Pearlman, New York.

GERMAN SCHOOL

OSKAR KOKOSCHKA 1886–

Bordeaux Cathedral

COLLECTION OF DR AND MRS THOMAS INGLEDOW, VANCOUVER

Kokoschka is probably the most individual of all the contemporary Expressionists. He was born at Pöchlarn in Austria and grew up mainly in Vienna, where he studied at the Kunstgewerbeschule from 1905 to 1909 and felt the influence of Gustav Klimt, Van Gogh, and Oriental art. He spent some time in Berlin on the staff of the advanced periodical *Der Sturm*, then returned to Vienna and taught at the Kunstgewerbeschule. He was wounded in the First World War and during his convalescence he met the poets Rainer Maria Rilke and Hugo von Hofmannsthal. In 1917 he moved to Dresden, where he studied the Old Masters at the Museum and taught at the Academy from 1919 to 1924. In 1925 he began his extensive travels in Europe and the Near East. When Hitler came to power he moved from Dresden to Prague, and his work was included in the exhibition of 'degenerate art' organized in Munich by the Nazis in 1937. In 1939 he fled to London before the German advance into Czechoslovakia. He visited the United States in 1949 and 1952–3, then settled on Lake Geneva in Switzerland. He is most widely known for his panoramic views of cities and his portraits of deep psychological penetration.

Bordeaux Cathedral was painted during Kokoschka's trip through south-western France at the end of 1924 or the beginning of 1925. It illustrates the intensity of his colour and the restless energy of his brushwork. Like all his paintings, it is emotionally charged and seems to express the pulsating life which he felt breathing over nature and the works of man. The picture was bought by the Nationalgalerie, Berlin, but was one of the many modern paintings removed from German museums by the Nazis and sold at auction in Lucerne in 1939.

Oil on canvas, 32″ × 24″.

LITERATURE

Westheim, *Kokoschka* (1925), supplement (after Pl. 99).
Hoffmann, *Kokoschka* (1947), p. 315, No. 165.
Wingler, *Kokoschka* (1958), p. 313, No. 175, reprod.

EXHIBITED
Berlin, Galerie Cassirer, 1925, No. 17.

EX COLLECTION
Nationalgalerie, Berlin (sale, Fischer, Lucerne, *Gemälde und Plastik moderner Meister aus deutschen Museen*, 1939, No. 64).

LV

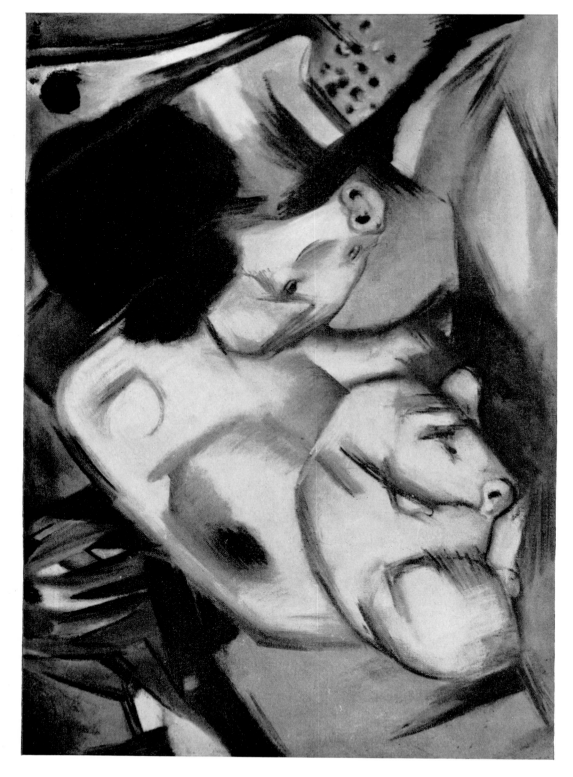

LVI

FRANZ MARC 1880-1916

Pigs

COLLECTION OF MR AND MRS FREDERICK MENDEL, SASKATOON

Franz Marc, one of the leaders of the German Expressionist movement, was born in Munich. At first he studied philosophy and theology but in 1900 he turned to painting and studied at the Munich Academy. He travelled to Italy in 1902, and in 1903-4 he visited Paris and Brittany, where he came into contact with the Impressionists and with Japanese art. In 1907 he met the animal painter Niestlé, who turned his attention to the subjects which were to become the most characteristic in his work. He went to Greece and Paris, where he underwent the critical influences of Van Gogh and Gauguin. In 1910 he met August Macke and Kandinsky in Munich and with them founded the Blaue Reiter group. The name was invented, according to Kandinsky, because both Marc and Kandinsky liked the colour blue, and because Marc liked to paint horses and Kandinsky riders. With the Dresden group, Die Brücke, they were responsible for the earliest important manifestation of modern art in Germany. Marc enlisted in the German army in 1914 and in 1916 made a series of abstract sketches before he fell in the Battle of Verdun.

This picture well illustrates Marc's way of arranging animal forms into simplified, expressive shapes, which in turn he organized into compositions that had sharp angles and 'lines of force'. His colour was electric in its intensity and has very brilliant highlights. The picture was painted about 1914.

Oil on canvas, $22\frac{3}{4}'' \times 32\frac{3}{4}''$.

EX COLLECTION
Schoen, Montreal.

EXHIBITED
Ottawa, National Gallery, *Mendel Collection*, 1955, No. 49, reprod. in cat.

GERMAN SCHOOL

KARL SCHMIDT-ROTTLUFF 1884-

Garten

COLLECTION OF DR AND MRS WILLIAM LANDMANN, TORONTO

With Kirchner and Erich Heckel, Schmidt-Rottluff was a leader of the Dresden group known as Die Brücke, who were active between 1905 and 1913. They and their Munich counterpart, the Blaue Reiter, were the great exponents of German Expressionism and the pioneers of modern painting in Germany. They were close in style to the Fauves in France and admired the work of Van Gogh, Gauguin, and the Norwegian expressionist Edvard Munch. Karl Schmidt was born at Rottluff, near Chemnitz in Saxony, the son of a miller, and later added the name of his birthplace to his own. He met Heckel in 1901 and with him visited museums and exhibitions. In 1905 he went to study architecture in Dresden, where he founded Die Brücke with Kirchner. He visited Norway in 1911 and there met the German-American painter Lyonel Feininger. He settled in Berlin, visiting Paris in 1924 and travelling to Dalmatia in 1925 and to Holland in 1935. His work was proscribed during the Nazi régime and was included in the exhibition of 'degenerate art' held at Munich in 1937. During the bombing of Berlin he moved to Rottluff but later returned to Berlin, where he now lives.

This landscape of 1919, with its emphatic and agitated black outlines and chord of intense colours, typifies the style of Schmidt-Rottluff's 'Numinous Period' of 1919–20. It also indicates the proximity of his style to that of the Fauves, for one is here reminded of the works of Dufy of the same period. But the energy—symbolized by the explosive shrub in the left foreground—offers a key to the essential character of this group, who inherited the long tradition of expressionism that began in the Middle Ages and extended through Dürer and the German Renaissance painters.

Oil on canvas, 28″ × 34″.

LITERATURE
Grohmann, *Schmidt-Rottluff* (1956), p. 290, reprod. p. 264.

EXHIBITED
Toronto, Art Gallery, 1946.

LVII

LVIII

GERMAN SCHOOL

OTTO DIX 1891–

Dr Stadelmann

COLLECTION OF DR AND MRS WILLIAM LANDMANN, TORONTO

Otto Dix was born at Gera in Saxony, the son of a foundry worker. He had his first art lessons at the Kunstgewerbeschule in Dresden, between 1909 and 1914. He was inspired by a Van Gogh exhibition which he saw in Dresden in 1913 and by the works of the German Primitives and the painters of the Jugendstil movement. But the greatest influence upon him was his experience in the First World War, when he made sketches at the front. After the war he returned to Dresden and studied painting at the Academy. He was interested in the social revolution going on about him and took his subjects from the chaotic life of the twenties. He participated in the Neue Sachlichkeit movement, which arose about 1920 in reaction to Expressionism, and he developed a personal style characterized by merciless realism and biting satire. In 1922 he left Dresden for Düsseldorf; in 1924 he visited Italy; and in 1925 he settled in Berlin. Later, from 1927 to 1933, he again lived in Dresden. When the Nazis came to power he retired to the country, and his paintings were removed from German museums. In 1939 he was arrested by the Gestapo on suspicion that he was a member of the underground but was later released.

The quality of Dix's style, which extended beyond realism to surrealism, appears in his portraits as well as in his better-known scenes of city life. It is well illustrated in this portrait with its curious expression of tingling life. In this respect it recalls the style of older German painters such as Grünewald.

Oil on canvas, $37\frac{1}{4}'' \times 26\frac{1}{2}''$.

BRITISH SCHOOL

RICHARD PARKES BONINGTON 1802–1828

View over the Solent

COLLECTION OF ROBERT W. REFORD, OTTAWA

Bonington was one of the leading masters of landscape painting in the early nineteenth century. He was born at Arnold near Nottingham. In 1818 he was at the École des Beaux-Arts in Paris and then in the studio of Baron Gros (who had modified the classic style of Jacques-Louis David in the direction of romanticism). His career was very short—he began to exhibit in 1822 and died six years later, before his twenty-sixth birthday. A trip to Venice in 1826 to see the Venetian masters influenced his painting considerably, chiefly in the style of his historical subjects. His landscapes, however, were more properly the products of his own skill. They were painted mostly in the coastal regions of northern France and southern England. Delacroix, with whom he used to copy the Old Masters in the Louvre, esteemed him highly as a landscape painter and called him a 'king in your own domain'. He died in London.

This Isle of Wight scene is one of Bonington's fine English landscapes, in which his delicate response to natural beauty may be clearly appreciated. Its tones are as transparent as those of a water colour, that distinctive medium of English landscape artists. Here may also be seen his typical lightness and grace and the grandiose impression of space which he conveyed. Here too are his limpid colours and his mastery in the handling of the brush. The picture is one of a collection of Boningtons made by the late R. W. Reford of Montreal, the grandfather of the present owner.

Oil on canvas, $13\frac{1}{2}'' \times 17''$.

EXHIBITED

Montreal, Art Association, *19th Century Landscape*, 1939, No. 2.

Toronto, Art Gallery, *Great Paintings*, 1940, No. 67.
Montreal, Museum, *Canada Collects*, 1960, No. 84.

EX COLLECTION

R. W. Reford, Montreal.

LIX

LX

WILLIAM HOLMAN HUNT 1827–1910

Henry Wentworth Monk

THE NATIONAL GALLERY OF CANADA

Holman Hunt, a leader of the Pre-Raphaelite movement in England, was born in London. At first he worked as a clerk in an estate office but later studied the collections in the British Museum and the National Gallery. At the Royal Academy Schools in 1844 he met Millais and Rossetti and with them formed the Pre-Raphaelite Brotherhood in 1848. The group was committed to truth to nature and to the expression of religious feeling in art. In carrying these ideals out they turned for inspiration to the period preceding Raphael and the High Renaissance and were much encouraged by Ruskin. That they succumbed however to the prevailing sentimentalism of the nineteenth century is abundantly clear in their later pictures. Of them all Hunt remained the most faithful to Pre-Raphaelite principles throughout his life. To achieve realism in his biblical subjects he travelled to Palestine in 1854–5, and to Florence, Rome, Naples, Alexandria, and Jerusalem in 1869. He was again in Jerusalem in 1873 and made further Eastern trips in 1876–7 and in 1892. He died in London.

Hunt met the extraordinary man in this portrait on his first trip to Palestine. By this time Henry Wentworth Monk (1827–1896) was already an advocate of universal peace, world government, and Zionism. Tradition has it that they met in the hills at sunrise. The sight of the young bearded figure standing in the half-light in a gateway sent Hunt's mind spinning back to the picture which he had painted in England the previous year, *The Light of the World*. Monk was accepted for a time by Hunt and Ruskin as the prophet of the age. On one occasion he visited Lincoln in order to stop the American Civil War. He had been born on a farm at South March near Ottawa of an English family who had settled there after the Napoleonic Wars and was educated at Christ's Hospital in London. In later life he was a familiar figure on Parliament Hill, Ottawa, where he communicated his ideas to anyone who would listen. The portrait was painted in 1858 and is full of symbolism, representing him in Eastern dress and holding in one hand a Greek New Testament (a reference to his preoccupation with the Book of Revelation) and in the other a copy of *The Times* (the present in which the prophecies were to come true).   Oil on canvas, 20" × 26".

LITERATURE
Hunt, *Pre-Raphaelitism and the Pre-Raphaelite Brotherhood* (1905), i, pp. 433–5, reprod. p. 433.
Schleinitz, *Hunt* (1907), pp. 45, Pl. 46.
Lambert, *For the Time is at Hand* (1947), p. 69, reprod. as frontispiece.
Hubbard, *National Gallery of Canada Catalogue*, ii (1959), pp. 86–7, reprod. p. 87.

EXHIBITED
London, Royal Academy, 1860, No. 510.
Toronto, Art Gallery, *Paintings from the National Gallery of Canada*, 1919, No. 38.

Pittsburgh, Carnegie Institute, *Paintings from the National Gallery of Canada*, 1919, No. 44.
Toronto, Art Gallery, *Portraits*, 1927, No. 49.
Windsor, Ontario, Willistead Art Gallery, 1946.
London, Ontario, Art Museum, 1946.
Winnipeg, Art Gallery, *Portraits*, 1956, No. 54.
New York, Jewish Museum, 1960.
Washington, B'nai Brith Museum, 1961.

EX COLLECTION
Mrs Edith Holman Hunt, London.
Acquired by the National Gallery of Canada, 1911.

DANTE GABRIEL ROSSETTI 1828-1882

Salutatio Beatricis

THE NATIONAL GALLERY OF CANADA

Dante Gabriel Rossetti was born in London, the son of a Dante scholar who was a political refugee from Italy; his mother was English. He studied painting first at Sass's School and then at the Royal Academy Schools. After a few months with Ford Madox Brown in 1848 he went to share a studio with Holman Hunt. In the same year he formed the Pre-Raphaelite Brotherhood with Hunt and Millais. He exhibited his first Pre-Raphaelite picture in 1849, but from the start his style stood out from that of the others in the group by its pronounced sensuousness. Taking his subjects largely from Dante, he created a medieval dream world for both his paintings and his poems. In 1850 he met Elizabeth Siddall, who had posed for Millais and Hunt, and painted her as model for *Beata Beatrix* and other pictures. He married her in 1860, and their unstable relationship seemed to stimulate the production of his best work. After her death from narcotics in 1862 he became something of a recluse. He died at Birchington-on-Sea.

Salutatio Beatricis is a diptych, painted in 1859, showing two meetings of Dante and Beatrice. At left is Dante's first sight of his love, and the frame is inscribed with lines from the *Vita Nuova*: 'Questa mirabile Donna apparve a me, vestita di colore bianco, in mezzo di due gentili donne di piu lunga etade.' At right is a scene from the *Purgatorio*: 'Sovra candido vel cinta d'uliva, Donna m'apparve sotto verde manto Vestita di color di fiamma viva.' The frame is an original one decorated by Rossetti.

Oil on two panels, each 29½″ × 31½″.

LITERATURE
Marillier, *Rossetti* (1901), pp. 25, 63, 86–88, 241, No. 89.

EXHIBITED
London, Royal Academy, *Loan Exhibition*, 1883, No. 289.
Rome, International Exhibition, 1911.

EX COLLECTION
James Leathart.
Acquired by the National Gallery of Canada, 1957.

LXI

LXII

WALTER RICHARD SICKERT 1860–1942

The Old Bedford: Cupid in the Gallery

THE NATIONAL GALLERY OF CANADA

Sickert, the leading English Impressionist, was born in Munich. His father was the Danish painter, Oswald Sickert, and his mother the daughter of an Irish dancer. The family settled in London in 1868. Sickert entered the Slade School in 1881 and the next year became a pupil of Whistler. In 1883 he went to Paris and was deeply influenced by Degas. After his divorce from his first wife in 1899 he left London and lived at Dieppe from 1900 to 1905, then returned to London. From 1907 to 1914 he lived in Camden Town and painted many pictures on the 'man and woman' theme. He went to Chagford in 1915 and lived at Bath in 1916–17. After the war he again lived at Dieppe, returning to England in 1922. His periodic visits to Venice began in 1895. He was a member of the New English Art Club in 1888 and was a founder of the Camden Town Group in 1911 and of the London Group in 1919. In the thirties he was in serious financial difficulties and was helped by Lord Beaverbrook and others who commissioned a number of large portraits. He resigned from the Royal Academy in 1935, and his protest against academic painting had widespread effects. In 1938 he moved to Bath, where he taught at the Academy and where he died.

The Old Bedford was painted in 1889 or 1890. At this time Sickert was living at Hampstead and would spend his evenings in restaurants or music halls. The Old Bedford, a music hall, burned in 1899 and was replaced by the New Bedford, which Sickert also painted. A number of versions of this painting exist, including those in the Fitzwilliam Museum in Cambridge and the Walker Art Gallery in Liverpool. The National Gallery canvas is the largest of the series. It is an example of his 'accidental' compositions in the manner of Degas, for it does not include the stage but only a small segment of the gallery. From the faces of the audience it is evident that he identified himself more personally with his human subjects than did Degas. Sickert's sombre palette is illustrated here, but the flashes of bright colour gleaming out from the dark background suit the subject perfectly.

Oil on canvas, 50″ × 30½″.

LITERATURE
Studio, xcviii (1929), reprod. p. 597.
Emmons, *Sickert* (1941), reprod. opp. p. 136.
Browse, *Sickert* (1943), p. 36.
Wilenski, *English Painting* (1943), Pl. 89.
Browse, *Sickert* (1960), pp. 65, 87.

EXHIBITED
London, Thomas Agnew & Son, *Sickert*, 1933, No. 3.
Amsterdam, Stedelijk Museum, *British Art*, 1936, No. 134.
New York, World's Fair, 1939, *Contemporary British Art*, No. 115.

London, Tate Gallery, *Massey Collection*, 1946, No. 52.
Ottawa, National Gallery, &c., *Massey Collection*, 1946, No. 54.
Sydney, National Gallery of New South Wales, &c., *Massey Collection*, 1949, No. 62, reprod. in cat.
Hamilton, Art Gallery, *Massey Collection*, 1954.

EX COLLECTION
Mrs A. B. Clifton.
The Rt Hon. Vincent Massey, C.H.
Presented to the National Gallery of Canada, 1946, by the Massey Foundation as a part of the Massey Collection of English Painting.

AUGUSTUS JOHN 1879-1961

Portrait of the Marchesa Casati

THE ART GALLERY OF TORONTO

Augustus John was one of the most brilliant exponents of portrait painting, which has always been an important aspect of English art. His career illustrates the development of an individual talent of high order. Born at Tenby, Pembrokeshire, he studied at the Liverpool Academy and at the Slade School in London. From 1900 to 1902 he taught at the Liverpool Academy, but returned to London where he joined the New English Art Club in 1903. In this early period he painted the gipsies of Wales and the fishermen of Connemara, and between 1911 and 1914 made painting trips with James Dickson Innes. He was influenced at this time by Puvis de Chavannes and the Impressionists, and made several large mural cartoons that demonstrated his mastery of line. He travelled widely in England and Europe. When he turned to portrait painting he was influenced to some degree by El Greco, Goya, and Rembrandt. In 1918 he worked for the Canadian War Memorials, making an immense charcoal cartoon with many figures for a proposed mural which was to commemorate the Canadians in the First World War but was never carried out. As a passionate opponent of academism in art he resigned from the Royal Academy in 1938 only to be reinstated in 1946. He was given the Order of Merit in 1942. He lived at Fordingbridge, Hampshire, until his death in 1961.

The Marchesa Casati was one of Augustus John's most famous sitters. He first met her at a reception in Paris at the time of the Peace Conference in 1919 and wrote of her in his journal: 'Her bearing, personality, and peculiar elegance seemed to throw the rest of the company into the shade. . . . Enormous eyes, set off by mascara, gleamed beneath a framework of canary-coloured curls.' The portrait illustrates the dash and grandeur of his mode of expression and his mastery of the brush. Another portrait of the Marchesa is in the collection of the Hon. Mary Sturt.

Oil on canvas, 38″ × 27″.

LITERATURE

Augustus John (1923), Pl. 16.
Canadian Art, v (1948), reprod. in colour, p. 165.
John, *Chiaroscuro* (1952), pp. 239–40.
Art Gallery of Toronto, *Illustrations* (1959), reprod.
  p. 47.

EXHIBITED

Toronto, Art Gallery, *Loan Exhibition*, 1935, No. 53.
Toronto, Art Gallery, *Great Paintings*, 1940, No. 86.
New York, Museum of Modern Art, *Twentieth Century Portraits*, 1942.
Toledo, Museum, 1948.

EX COLLECTION

Sir Evan Charteris, London (1934).
Acquired by the Art Gallery of Toronto, 1934.

LXIII

LXIV

BRITISH SCHOOL

SIR MATTHEW SMITH 1879–1959

Bouquet of Flowers

THE NATIONAL GALLERY OF CANADA

Matthew Smith has rightly been described as the English Fauve, for he followed Fauvist principles all his life. He was born at Halifax, Yorkshire, and was taken into his father's wire factory at an early age. In 1905, however, he was allowed to go to London and to study painting at the Slade School. In 1908 he went to paint in Brittany and stayed some months at Pont-Aven where, he said, 'my mind began to open out'. A little later he painted at Étaples and arrived in Paris in 1910, where he studied briefly at Matisse's school. After travelling again in Europe he returned to England and became a member of the London Group. In 1920 he painted a series of landscapes of Cornwall in which he developed the vigorous and opulent technique that is the chief characteristic of his style. This trend continued during his travels back and forth between England and France in the twenties and thirties. He lived at Aix-en-Provence from 1934 until he returned to England at the outbreak of war. He was knighted in 1954 and died in London.

This flower-piece was given to the National Gallery of Canada by the Birmingham collector James Archdale, who deposited his pictures in the Gallery during the Second World War. It well exemplifies Matthew Smith's intensification of Fauve colour, but in spite of its lavishness it is one of his more disciplined compositions.

Oil on canvas, 26″ × 21¾″.

LITERATURE
Hubbard, *National Gallery of Canada Catalogue*, ii (1959), p. 144, reprod.

EXHIBITED
Winnipeg, Art Gallery, 1949.
Regina, Exhibition Association, 1949.
Montreal, Museum, *National Gallery of Canada Collection*, 1949.
Presented to the National Gallery of Canada, 1946, by James Archdale, Birmingham.

HAROLD GILMAN 1876-1919

Halifax Harbour at Sunset

THE NATIONAL GALLERY OF CANADA

Harold Gilman was born at Rodd, Somerset, the son of a clergyman. He spent a year at Oxford but turned to painting and studied at the Hastings Art School in 1896 and the Slade School, London, in 1897. In 1904 he went to Spain and studied the works of Velasquez and Goya in the museums. On his return to London he joined the artistic circle of Walter Richard Sickert, but his greatest stimulation came from the Post-Impressionist exhibition of 1910 in London. Under the influence of Gauguin and Signac in particular he reacted against Impressionism, adopted a brighter palette, and made bold designs of the separate brushstrokes on the surface of the canvas. He helped to found the Camden Town Group in 1911 and was the first president of the London Group at its foundation in 1913. He died in London.

This mural-size picture of Halifax Harbour in wartime was painted in 1918 for the Canadian War Memorials. A late work of Gilman, it epitomizes his mature style by its breadth of composition, emphatic brushwork, and radiant colours.

Oil on canvas, 77″ × 132″.

LITERATURE
Lewis and Ferguson, *Gilman* (1919), pp. 31–32.
Rothenstein, *Modern English Painters*, i (1952), p. 154.
Hubbard, *National Gallery of Canada Catalogue*, ii (1959), p. 211, reprod.

EXHIBITED
London, Royal Academy, *Canadian War Memorials*, 1919.
New York, Anderson Galleries, &c., *Canadian War Memorials*, 1919, No. 5.
Ottawa, National Gallery, *Canadian War Memorials*, 1923, No. 13.
Toronto, Art Gallery, *Canadian War Memorials*, 1926, No. 62.
Deposited in the National Gallery of Canada, 1920.

LXV

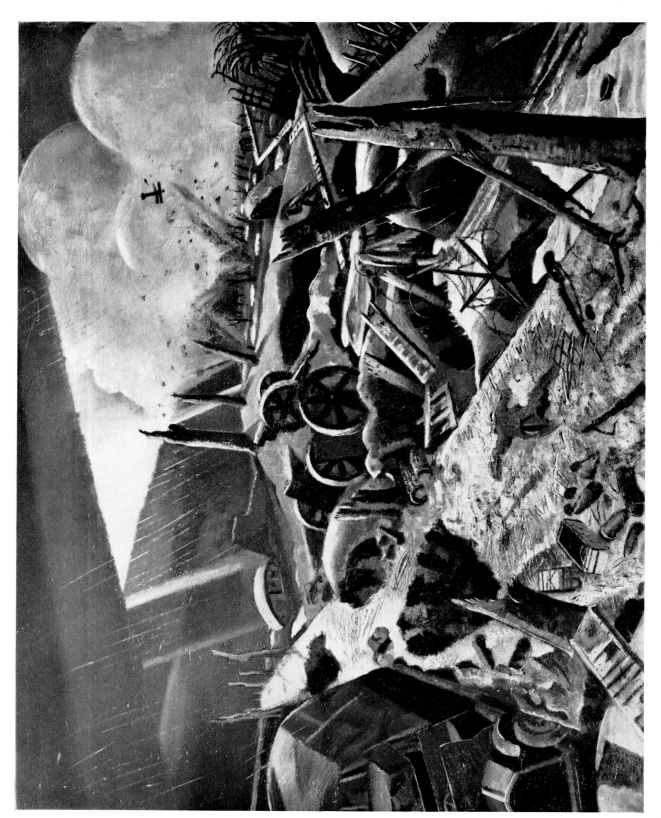

LXVI

PAUL NASH 1889–1946

Void

THE NATIONAL GALLERY OF CANADA

Paul Nash was born in London but moved to Iver Heath, Buckinghamshire, in 1901. After St Paul's School he attended evening art classes in London from 1906 to 1909 and studied at the Slade School from 1910 to 1912. In 1914 he worked under Roger Fry and at the restoration of the Mantegna cartoons at Hampton Court. The same year he enlisted in the Artists' Rifles and was made an official war artist in 1917. In 1918 he painted for the Canadian War Memorials. After the war he lived at Dymchurch, Kent, and in 1924–5 taught at the Royal College of Art in London. In 1933–4 he travelled to Europe and North Africa; he settled at Oxford in 1937. His poetic imagination was stimulated by the Surrealists and in 1938 he exhibited with them in Paris. During the Second World War he was an official war artist to the Air Ministry. He also worked as an illustrator, designer, and graphic artist. He died in London.

Void, painted in 1918 for the Canadian War Memorials, is one of the finest and most characteristic works from Nash's early period. Using the chaotic forms of the battlefield and its livid colours, he 'distilled a new poetry, sombre yet beautiful'. He was able to express the horror and destruction of war better than any other artist of his time. In one of his letters he described a scene such as this: 'The most frightful nightmare of a country conceived by Dante or Poe. . . . Sunset and sunrise are blasphemous to man . . . the black rain out of the bruised and swollen clouds . . . the yellow mud, the green-white water, the shattered tree trunks.'

Oil on canvas, 28″ × 36″.

LITERATURE
Eates, *Nash* (1948), p. 74.
Hubbard, *National Gallery of Canada Catalogue*, ii (1959), p. 213, reprod.

EXHIBITED
London, Royal Academy, *Canadian War Memorials*, 1919.

New York, Anderson Galleries, &c., *Canadian War Memorials*, 1919, No. 74.
Ottawa, National Gallery, *Canadian War Memorials*, 1923, No. 74.
Toronto, Art Gallery, *Canadian War Memorials*, 1926, No. 158.
Toronto, Canadian National Exhibition, 1949.
Deposited in the National Gallery of Canada, 1920.

PAUL NASH 1889-1946

Solstice of the Sunflower

THE NATIONAL GALLERY OF CANADA

This late work of Paul Nash, painted the year before his death, is the climax of his development. It is a rhapsody on the dynamic of nature with an almost Blake-like intensity of feeling. Nash apparently adopted the sunflower as his symbol of nature after finding it used as an image by two of his favourite authors, Sir Thomas Browne and William Blake:

> Ah, Sunflower! weary of time,
> Who countest the steps of the sun . . .
>
> BLAKE

Oil on canvas, 28″ × 36″.

LITERATURE

Eates, *Nash* (1948), p. 78, reprod. in colour, Pl. 115.
Architectural Review, ciii (1948), p. 117, reprod. in colour.
Canadian Art, x (1953), p. 47, reprod. in colour.
Bertram, *Nash* (1955), pp. 169, 300–2, Pl. 32.
Hubbard, *National Gallery of Canada Catalogue*, ii (1959), p. 117, reprod.

EXHIBITED

London, Tooth & Son, 1945, 1946.
London, Tate Gallery, *Nash*, 1948, No. 67.
Winnipeg, Art Gallery, 1955.

EX COLLECTION

R. M. D. Thesiger, London.
The Rt Hon. Vincent Massey, C.H.
Presented to the National Gallery of Canada, 1952, by the Massey Foundation as part of the Massey Collection of English Painting.

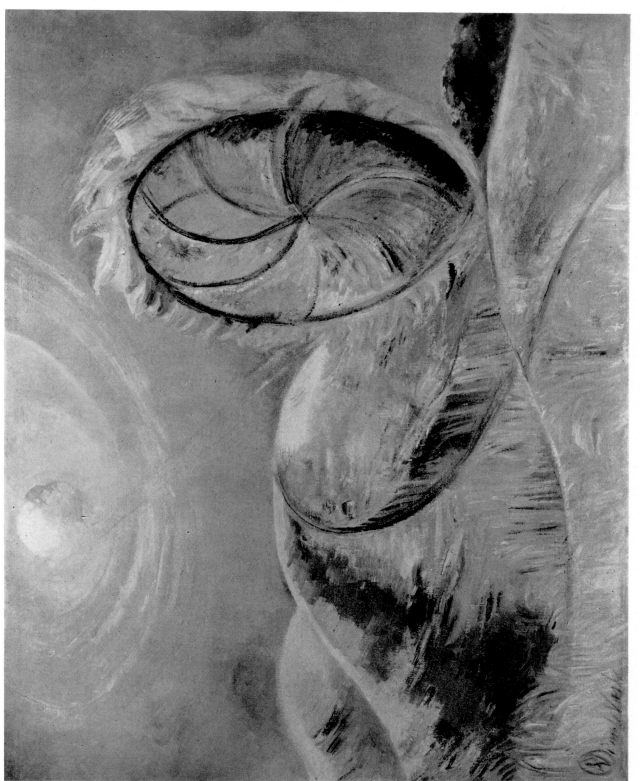

LXVII

SIR STANLEY SPENCER 1891–1959

Marsh Meadows, Cookham

THE NATIONAL GALLERY OF CANADA

Born at Cookham, Berkshire, Stanley Spencer was the son of a local organist and music teacher. He studied at the Slade School in London and exhibited at the second Post-Impressionist exhibition in London in 1912. Early in his career he began a series of biblical subjects, the style of which was influenced by the Italian Primitives and the English Pre-Raphaelites. After travels in Italy and Switzerland he served in the First World War with the Army Medical Corps in Macedonia, and his experiences there are recorded in a series of mural paintings for the Oratory of All Souls', Burghclere, between 1926 and 1932. He joined the New English Art Club in 1919. In 1923 he began a long series of paintings of the Resurrection. He was first elected to the Royal Academy in 1933; he resigned in 1935 but was re-elected in 1950. During the thirties he was largely occupied with landscapes of Cookham. He worked in London in 1938–9 and thereafter at various places until he retired to Cookham in 1945. During the Second World War he was commissioned to paint a series of shipyard subjects but after it he returned to his biblical themes which he interpreted in terms of English everyday life.

Marsh Meadows, Cookham, painted during the thirties in Spencer's native village on the Thames, is representative of his comprehending love of his own region. In true English fashion he looked closely at familiar places and things and carried on an old tradition in English painting. Like many older English artists too he showed great skill in drawing.

Oil on canvas, 25″ × 30″.

LITERATURE
Art Quarterly, ix (1946), reprod. p. 268.
Hubbard, *National Gallery of Canada Catalogue*, ii (1959), p. 146, reprod.

EXHIBITED
London, Tate Gallery, *Massey Collection*, 1946, No. 61.
Ottawa, National Gallery, &c., *Massey Collection*, 1946, No. 63, reprod. in cat.

Sydney, National Gallery of New South Wales, &c., *Massey Collection*, 1949, No. 71, reprod. in cat.
Hamilton, Art Gallery, *Massey Collection*, 1954.

EX COLLECTION
The Rt Hon. Vincent Massey, C.H.
Presented to the National Gallery of Canada, 1946, by the Massey Foundation as part of the Massey Collection of English Painting.

IVON HITCHENS 1893–

Forest End

THE NATIONAL GALLERY OF CANADA

Hitchens is one of the most characteristically English painters of the twentieth century, by virtue of a style that is individual and contemporary and yet continues the traditions of Turner, Constable, and the English Impressionists. His training was at the St John's Wood School of Art and the Royal Academy Schools, London, but the strongest influence upon him in his early life was that of Matisse. Whereas in Matthew Smith the impact of Matisse had resulted in a riot of colour, it inspired in Hitchens a decorative and lyric style. He became a member of the London Group and the Seven and Five Group. His work was shown in the British pavilion at the Venice Biennale of 1956.

Hitchens lives at Petworth, where Turner painted some of his most impressionistic landscapes and interiors. *Forest End*, with its autumnal colour harmonies, has much of the curiously English quality of Turner's works—a gentleness combined with a deep poetic feeling.

Oil on canvas, 16″ × 29⅜″.

LITERATURE
Hubbard, *National Gallery of Canada Catalogue*, ii (1959), p. 85, reprod.

EXHIBITED
London, Tate Gallery, *Massey Collection*, 1946, No. 12.
Ottawa, National Gallery, &c., *Massey Collection*, 1946, No. 14.

Sydney, National Gallery of New South Wales, &c., *Massey Collection*, 1949, No. 15, reprod. in cat.

EX COLLECTION
The Rt Hon. Vincent Massey, C.H.
Presented to the National Gallery of Canada, 1946, by the Massey Foundation as part of the Massey Collection of English Painting.

LXIX

BEN NICHOLSON 1894–

Still Life (Abelard and Heloise)

THE NATIONAL GALLERY OF CANADA

Ben Nicholson was born at Denham, Buckinghamshire, the eldest son of the painter Sir William Nicholson (1872–1949). His mother was the sister of the Scottish artist James Pryde. He studied briefly in 1910–11 at the Slade School, London, but was mainly self-taught. In his youth he travelled widely, going to Tours in 1911–12 to learn French, to Milan in 1912–13 to study Italian, to Madeira in 1913–14, and to California for his health in 1917–18. He spent much time in Switzerland between 1920 and 1931. The development of his style was influenced by Picasso, Braque, Miró, and Mondrian. In 1939 he settled in Cornwall and now lives at St Ives. His work was shown in the British pavilion at the Venice Biennale of 1954, and he was the first winner of the Guggenheim International Award for painting.

The sub-title of this picture, *Abelard and Heloise*, was perhaps given because the chaste and closely interwoven forms reminded the artist of the relationship of these two famous figures in medieval history. It is a large and important picture of 1950, illustrating Ben Nicholson's severely geometric style. It also shows the fastidiousness of his technique, and what may be called an English interpretation of abstraction.

Oil on canvas, $47\frac{1}{8}'' \times 65\frac{1}{8}''$.

LITERATURE

Read, *Nicholson*, ii (1956), Pl. 6.
Hubbard, *National Gallery of Canada Catalogue*, ii (1959), p. 120, reprod.

EXHIBITED

Ottawa, National Gallery, &c., *Five Contemporary British Painters*, 1952, No. 28, reprod. in cat.
Winnipeg, Art Gallery, 1955, 1957.
Regina, Mackenzie Art Gallery, 1956.
Acquired by the National Gallery of Canada, 1953.

A CHECKLIST OF
SELECTED EUROPEAN PAINTINGS
IN CANADIAN COLLECTIONS

NOTE: *Unless otherwise indicated, the medium is oil on canvas. Measurements are in inches. Titles are given in their original languages wherever known. The works marked with a star are illustrated in this book, and full references for these are given on the pages facing the illustrations. Full references to pictures in the Montreal Museum of Fine Arts and the National Gallery of Canada may be found in the catalogues of these institutions.*

ABBREVIATIONS

A.G.	Art Gallery	Mus.	Museum
attr.	attributed	N.G.C.	The National Gallery of Canada, Ottawa
B.	board	P.	panel
c.	*circa*	Pl.	plate
cat.	catalogue	S.	signed
D.	dated	Ref.	reference
G.	gouache	W.	watercolour

FRENCH SCHOOL
(including some painters of the School of Paris)

PIERRE BONNARD, 1867–1947

Blonde nu. 24½ × 18½. S. Ref.: Beer, *Bonnard* (1947), Pl. 80. Montreal, Lazarus Phillips.

Les deux fiacres. 17½ × 29. S. Winnipeg, J. A. MacAulay.

Esterel vu du Cannet (*c.* 1939). 25½ × 22. S. Toronto, John David Eaton.

Nature morte: pommes. 12 × 16. S. Montreal, Maxwell Cummings.

Neige (1907). 13¼ × 17¾. S. Ref.: Werth, *Bonnard* (n.d.), Pl. 3. Montreal, Lazarus Phillips.

Paysage. 13¾ × 17¼. S. Toronto, Gerald Larkin.

Paysage à Vernon (1919). 18¾ × 30¾. S. Winnipeg, J. A. MacAulay.

Paysage avec chaumière. 21¾ × 26½. S. Winnipeg, J. A. MacAulay.

Paysage de neige. W. 10⅞ × 8⅝. Montreal, L. V. Randall.

Paysage du Midi (1916–18). 53¾ × 78. S. Toronto, Samuel Zacks.

★Le Port de Cannes. 16½ × 26. S. Ottawa, N.G.C.

★La Table garnie (*c.* 1924), 14½ × 21½. S. Toronto, A.G.

EUGÈNE-LOUIS BOUDIN, 1824–1898

Bateaux dans une rivière. P., 14 × 11. Montreal, E. B. Hosmer estate.

Bateaux dans une rivière. 18 × 25½. S. Montreal, Mrs I. A. Chipman.

Bateaux de pêche à Douarnenez (1897). 21½ × 35½. S.D. Winnipeg, R. A. Purves.

Bateaux sur une plage (1875). 14 × 22¾. S.D. Montreal, Murray Vaughan.

Beaulieu: la baie (1892). 21¼ × 35½. S.D. Toronto, A.G.

Bordeaux. 29½ × 39½. S. Toronto, A.G.

La Cale de Radoub, à Bordeaux (1878). 19 × 29. S.D. Toronto, A.G.

Un coin de Louvain (1871). P., 15¼ × 23. S. Montreal, Mrs William Van Horne.

La Croisée. 14½ × 23. Edmonton, E. E. Poole.

Deauville: la gare (1880). 10¾ × 16¼. S.D. Montreal, E. B. Hosmer estate.

Deux vaches en repos. 5⅜ × 9½. S. Saskatoon, Frederick Mendel.

La fête de Sainte-Anne (1858). P., 13½ × 16¼. S.D. Montreal, E. B. Hosmer estate.

La Gouvernante, à Trouville (1870). 4¾ × 8½. S.D. Montreal, E. B. Hosmer estate.

A Harbour (1890). P., 10¾ × 8¾. S.D. Montreal, Lazarus Phillips.

A Harbour (1892). 16¼ × 21¾. S.D. Montreal, Mus.

[149]

Honfleur. $7\frac{1}{2} \times 10\frac{3}{4}$. S. Vancouver, Mrs J. P. Fell.

La Jetée de Trouville. P., 8×11. Vancouver, Mrs J. P. Fell.

La Jetée de Trouville (1864). $9 \times 14\frac{1}{2}$. S.D. Montreal, E. B. Hosmer estate.

La Jetée de Trouville (1864). $18\frac{1}{4} \times 25$. S.D. Montreal, E. B. Hosmer estate.

Le Havre (1894). $16 \times 21\frac{3}{4}$. S.D. Montreal, P. F. Osler.

Le Touquet (1895). $18 \times 25\frac{1}{2}$. S.D. Vancouver, Mrs B. T. Rogers.

The Market Place, Trouville (1890). $9\frac{3}{4} \times 13\frac{1}{2}$. Montreal, Mus.

Mill Stream. $21\frac{1}{2} \times 18\frac{1}{2}$. S. Montreal, Mrs I. A. Chipman.

Moonlight, Saint-Valéry (1891). P., $17\frac{1}{4} \times 14\frac{3}{8}$. S.D. Montreal, Miss Olive Hosmer.

Moulin à Dordrecht (1883). $19 \times 23\frac{1}{2}$. S.D. Montreal, Murray Vaughan.

Pardon: Church and Peasants. P., $13\frac{1}{2} \times 11$. Senneville, Que., Commander F. W. R. Angus.

Une Plage (1886). $14 \times 22\frac{1}{2}$. S.D. Montreal, E. B. Hosmer estate.

La Plage de Trouville. $14\frac{1}{2} \times 23$. S. Toronto, Mrs Glyn Osler.

Le Port d'Anvers. $16 \times 25\frac{3}{4}$. Montreal, P. F. Osler.

Le Port de Boulogne (1876). 21×29. S.D. Montreal, E. B. Hosmer estate.

Le Port de Rotterdam (1880). $30\frac{1}{2} \times 43$. S.D. Ottawa, Mrs Margaret Brinckman.

Portrait de Juliette (1895). P., $14 \times 9\frac{1}{2}$. S.D. Montreal, Murray Vaughan.

Régates à Anvers. $21\frac{1}{4} \times 35$. S. Vancouver, A.G.

Régates à Anvers (1871). P., $13\frac{1}{2} \times 24\frac{1}{4}$. S.D. Montreal, E. B. Hosmer estate.

The Sea (1885). $25\frac{1}{2} \times 35$. S.D. Montreal, Mus.

A Seaport. $10 \times 12\frac{1}{2}$. S. Vancouver, H. Mortimer Lamb.

A Seaport. $22 \times 33\frac{1}{2}$. Montreal, Samuel Bronfman.

Sea-shore (1880). $15\frac{1}{2} \times 22$. S.D. Montreal, Mus.

★Sur la plage à Trouville (1864). 26×40. Montreal, E. B. Hosmer estate.

Sur la plage à Trouville (c. 1864). $9 \times 15\frac{3}{4}$. S. Montreal, Murray Vaughan.

Sur la plage à Trouville (1869). P., $13\frac{1}{2} \times 22\frac{1}{2}$. S.D. Montreal, E. B. Hosmer estate.

Sur la plage à Trouville (1870). $11\frac{1}{2} \times 19$. S.D. Montreal, E. B. Hosmer estate.

Sur la plage à Trouville (1884). P., $6\frac{1}{2} \times 10\frac{3}{4}$. S.D. Montreal, E. B. Hosmer estate.

Sur la plage à Trouville: coucher du soleil. P., $14\frac{1}{4} \times 22\frac{1}{4}$. S. Montreal, E. B. Hosmer estate.

Trouville (1866). 16×25. S.D. Montreal, E. B. Hosmer estate.

Trouville (1867). 7×13. S.D. Montreal, Dr A. T. Henderson.

Trouville (1886). $9\frac{1}{2} \times 16$. S.D. Montreal, E. B. Hosmer estate.

Venice (1895). $9\frac{1}{2} \times 29$. S.D. Montreal, E. B. Hosmer estate.

Vue d'Étaples: la Marée basse (1886). $33 \times 50\frac{1}{2}$. Ref.: Benjamin, *Boudin* (1937), p. 178. Ottawa, N.G.C.

GEORGES BRAQUE, 1882–

Nature morte (1926). $8\frac{3}{4} \times 13$. S.D. Hamilton, A.G. (stolen 1960).

Paysage à L'Estaque (1906). 15×18. S. Ref.: Russell, *Braque* (1959), Pl. 4. Montreal, Lazarus Phillips.

Les Pêches (1929–30). $19\frac{3}{4} \times 25\frac{1}{2}$. S. Saskatoon, Frederick Mendel.

★Le Port d'Anvers (1906). $19\frac{5}{8} \times 24$. Ottawa, N.G.C.

Still Life with Apples and Jug (c. 1923). P., $9 \times 12\frac{3}{4}$. S. Toronto, Samuel Zacks.

Still Life with Grapes (1925). $8\frac{3}{4} \times 18\frac{1}{4}$. S. Toronto, David Meltzer.

Still Life with Playing Cards and Pipe (c. 1914). P., $7\frac{3}{4} \times 9\frac{3}{4}$. Toronto, Samuel Zacks.

★Vase gris et palette (1938). 42×35. Toronto, John David Eaton.

MARY CASSATT, 1845–1926

Head of a Girl in a Blue Hat (1895). Pastel. $26\frac{1}{4} \times 22\frac{1}{4}$. S. Toronto, David Meltzer.

Head of a Girl in a Straw Hat. Pastel. 17×21. S. Montreal, Samuel Bronfman.

Mother and Daughter. Pastel. 24×18. S. Montreal, Maxwell Cummings.

PAUL CÉZANNE, 1839–1906

Les Arbres (c. 1900). W. $18 \times 11\frac{3}{4}$. Ref.: *Burlington Magazine*, cii (1960), reprod. p. 116. Montreal, Lazarus Phillips.

Forêt (1902–4). 32×26. Ref.: Venturi, *Cézanne* (1936), No. 1530. Ottawa, N.G.C.

Fruits et casserole (1874–8). P., 20×24. S. Montreal, Mus.

Médan: château et village (c. 1885). $31\frac{1}{2} \times 25\frac{1}{2}$. Ref.: Venturi, No. 439. Winnipeg, J. A. MacAulay.

★Paysage (1879–82). $17\frac{3}{4} \times 21\frac{1}{4}$. Montreal, Mrs I. A. Chipman.

Portrait de Boyer (1870–1). 18×15. Ref.: Venturi, No. 132. Ottawa, N.G.C.

Portrait d'enfant (1883–7). Oil on paper. 11×13. Ref.: Venturi, No. 1521. Montreal, U. L. Steiner.

★Portrait de paysan (1900–4). $35\frac{3}{4} \times 29\frac{3}{4}$. Ottawa, N.G.C.

★Prairie et ferme du Jas de Bouffan (1885–7). $26 \times 32\frac{1}{2}$. Ottawa, N.G.C.

La Route à Auvers-sur-Oise (1873–4). $21\frac{5}{8} \times 18\frac{1}{8}$. Ref.: Venturi, No. 147. Ottawa, N.G.C.

Route tournante en Provence (1867–70). 36×28. Ref.: Venturi, No. 53. Montreal, Mus.

MARC CHAGALL, 1887–

L'Artiste et son modèle. G., $27\frac{3}{4} \times 20$. S. Ottawa, N.G.C.

★Au-dessus de Vitebsk (1914). Oil on paper. $27\frac{1}{2} \times 35\frac{1}{4}$. Toronto, Samuel Zacks.

Bride and Groom. $19\frac{1}{2} \times 15$. S. Montreal, Lazarus Phillips.

Cheval bleu au double face (1947–50). 26 × 20. S. Ref.: Estienne, *Chagall* (1951), reprod. p. 81. Saskatoon, Frederick Mendel.

Le Corbeil au couteau (1932). G., $24\frac{1}{2} \times 19\frac{1}{4}$. S.D. Winnipeg, J. A. MacAulay.

La Crépuscule. G., $25\frac{3}{8} \times 19\frac{1}{2}$. Winnipeg, P. D. Curry.

En avant!: curtain design for a play by Gogol (1917). G., $15 \times 19\frac{1}{4}$. S.D. Ref.: Venturi, reprod. in colour, p. 56. Toronto, Samuel Zacks.

Une fable de La Fontaine. G., $19\frac{3}{4} \times 15\frac{3}{4}$. Winnipeg, Dr S. Kobrinsky.

La Ferme (*c.* 1920). $14\frac{1}{4} \times 14$. S. St Andrews East, Que., Mrs L. T. Porter.

My Youth (*c.* 1923). $29\frac{1}{4} \times 34$. Toronto, Dr William Landmann.

Still Life with Flowers and Lovers. G., $29\frac{1}{2} \times 22\frac{1}{8}$. S. Winnipeg, A.G.

La Tour Eiffel (1923). $39\frac{5}{8} \times 32$. S. Ottawa, N.G.C.

Temptation (1911). $9\frac{1}{2} \times 13\frac{1}{2}$. S.D. Montreal, Murray Vaughan.

JEAN-BAPTISTE-CAMILLE COROT, 1796–1875

Auvers—une rue descendante (1865). P., $16\frac{1}{4} \times 9\frac{1}{2}$. S. Ref.: Robaut, *Corot* (1905), No. 1308. Ottawa, N.G.C.

Baigneuses dans une crique boisée (1855–7). $10\frac{1}{2} \times 13\frac{3}{4}$. S. Ref.: Robaut, No. 1182. Ottawa, Lady Brinckman.

Coubron—cour d'une maison de paysans (1873). 22 × 18. S. Ref.: Robaut, No. 2176. Montreal, Mrs J. C. McDougall.

La Dune de Dunkerque (1873). P., $14\frac{1}{2} \times 26\frac{1}{2}$. S. Ref.: Robaut, No. 2121. Montreal, Mrs William Van Horne.

Une ferme de Dardagny (1850–60). $16\frac{1}{2} \times 13\frac{3}{4}$. S. Ref.: Robaut, No. 721. Montreal, E. B. Hosmer estate.

Fontainebleau—grès dans la lande (1845–50). 10 × 15. Ref. : Robaut, No. 492. Vancouver, Mrs J. P. Fell.

Les Gaulois (1874). 22 × 26. S. Ref.: Robaut, No. 2310. Montreal, Mus.

Groupe d'arbres au bord d'un marais, avec deux vaches (soleil levant) (1865–70). $18\frac{1}{4} \times 21\frac{1}{2}$. S. Ref.: Robaut, No. 1894. Winnipeg, R. A. Purves.

*L'Île heureuse (1865–8). $73 \times 55\frac{1}{2}$. Montreal, Mus.

Jeune femme accoudée sur le bras gauche (*c.* 1865). $18\frac{1}{4} \times 15$. Ref.: Robaut, No. 1340. Montreal, Miss Olive Hosmer.

Mlle Louise Audiat costumée à l'antique (1852). $15\frac{1}{2} \times 10\frac{1}{2}$. Ref.: Robaut, No. 1049. Montreal, Mus.

Maisons au bord de l'eau (1855–65). P., $13\frac{3}{4} \times 20\frac{1}{4}$. Ref.: Robaut, No. 1004. Winnipeg, J. A. MacAulay.

La petite curieuse (1850–60). B., $16\frac{1}{2} \times 11$. S. Ref.: Robaut, No. 1042. Montreal, Mrs William Van Horne.

*Le pont de Narni (1826–7). $26\frac{3}{4} \times 37\frac{1}{4}$. Ottawa, N.G.C.

La Prairie aux deux gros arbres (1865–70). $17\frac{1}{4} \times 23\frac{3}{4}$. S. Ref.: Robaut, No. 1892. Toronto, C. S. Band.

La Rencontre au bord du chemin (1872–3). $18 \times 29\frac{1}{2}$. S. Ref.: Robaut, No. 2270. Montreal, Samuel Bronfman.

La Rêveuse à la fontaine (1860–70). $25 \times 17\frac{1}{4}$. S. Ref.: Robaut, No. 1342. Montreal, Mrs W. F. Angus.

Route à l'entrée d'un bois, avec un cavalier et une paysanne (1860–70). $21\frac{1}{2} \times 14$. S. Ref.: Robaut, No. 1796. Montreal, Murray Vaughan.

La Solitude—souvenir de Vigen (1873). $37\frac{3}{4} \times 43\frac{3}{4}$. Ref.: Robaut, No. 1638*ter.* Montreal, Oskar Federer.

Souvenir de la plage de Biarritz (1874). $15\frac{3}{4} \times 21\frac{3}{4}$. S. Ref.: Robaut, No. 2408. Montreal, Mrs Howard W. Pillow.

Le Tibre près de Rome (1826–8). B., $8\frac{1}{2} \times 13\frac{1}{4}$. Ref.: Robaut, No. 76. Montreal, Lazarus Phillips.

Ville d'Avray—Le pêcheur auprès de l'écluse (1852). $15 \times 18\frac{1}{2}$. S. Ref.: Robaut, No. 680. Montreal, Frederick Kahn.

GUSTAVE COURBET, 1819–1877

Les Cascades (*c.* 1865). $38\frac{1}{2} \times 50\frac{1}{2}$. S. Ref.: *Art Quarterly*, x (1947), p. 227. Ottawa, N.G.C.

Château de Chillon, en automne (*c.* 1875). $27\frac{1}{4} \times 37\frac{1}{2}$. Ottawa, Mrs C. Rowley Booth.

Chevreuils dans la neige (*c.* 1866). $13 \times 16\frac{1}{8}$. S. Montreal, Dr Max Stern.

*Dans le bois: neige (*c.* 1860–6). $23\frac{1}{2} \times 29$. Ottawa, N.G.C.

La femme aux gants. $24 \times 20\frac{1}{2}$. S. Ottawa, N.G.C.

Femme peinte à Palavas (1854). $23\frac{1}{4} \times 19$. S. Toronto, A.G.

Forêt. $19\frac{1}{2} \times 24\frac{1}{4}$. S. Montreal, Miss Olive Hosmer.

Landscape with Rocks and Stream (1872). 29 × 30. S.D. Montreal, Mus.

Marine (1866). $19\frac{1}{2} \times 39\frac{1}{2}$. S.D. Toronto, A.G.

Marine (*c.* 1866). $19\frac{3}{4} \times 24$. S. Montreal, P. F. Osler.

Nature morte à l'ail (1871). P., $6 \times 27\frac{3}{4}$. S.D. Toronto, Samuel Zacks.

Nature morte: fruits (1871). $9\frac{1}{2} \times 12\frac{3}{4}$. S.D. Montreal, Mrs William Van Horne.

Paysage près de Dinan. $28\frac{1}{2} \times 36\frac{1}{4}$. S. Montreal, P. F. Osler.

Pool in the Woods. $18 \times 21\frac{1}{2}$. S. Montreal, Mus.

The Poor Woman of the Village (1866). $33\frac{1}{2} \times 50$. S.D. Montreal, L. M. Bloomfield.

Le Puits noir (*c.* 1865). $21\frac{1}{4} \times 25\frac{1}{4}$. S. Hamilton, A.G. (stolen 1960).

Le Ruisseau du Puits noir (*c.* 1865). 25 × 22. S. Ref.: Muther, *Modern Art* (1896), p. 516, reprod. p. 522. Montreal, Mus.

*Les Rochers à Étretat (1866). 36 × 45. S.D. Ottawa, N.G.C.

Souvenir de guerre (1871). $12 \times 17\frac{1}{2}$. S.D. Winnipeg, Dr S. Kobrinsky.

CHARLES-FRANÇOIS DAUBIGNY, 1817–1878

Andressey-sur-Oise (1865). 14 × 25. S.D. Vancouver, Mrs B. T. Rogers.

The Breakwater (1872). P., $10\frac{1}{2} \times 18\frac{1}{2}$. S.D. Montreal, Mus.

Building the Stack. $19\frac{1}{4} \times 26$. S. Montreal, Mus.

Landscape. $9\frac{1}{2} \times 15\frac{1}{2}$. S. Ottawa, N.G.C.

On the Banks of the Oise (1886). P., $14\frac{3}{4} \times 26$. S.D. Montreal, Mus.

The Return of the Flock (1877). 42 × 74. Montreal, Mus.
The Storm. 21¼ × 33½. Toronto, H. G. Walker.
Sunset on a River (1869). 10 × 21. S.D. Toronto, A.G.
The Valley of the Dieppe (1871). 13 × 23. Montreal, Mus.

HONORÉ DAUMIER, 1808–1879

*Les Critiques (1856–65). W. 13¾ × 17¼. Ref.: Adhémar, *Daumier* (1954), reprod. in colour, Pl. 93. Montreal, Mus.
*Les Fugitifs (1848–9). P., 6¼ × 12¼. Montreal, Mrs William Van Horne.
L'Homme à la corde (1860–2). 32½ × 28½. Ottawa, N.G.C.
A Musical Party (attr.). P., 10 × 14. Montreal, Mrs William Van Horne.
*Nymphes poursuivies par des satyres (1849–50). 51¾ × 38¼. S. Ref.: Adhémar, reprod. in colour, Pl. 56. Montreal, Mus.
Street in Montmartre (attr.). 20¼ × 14. S. Ref.: Tietze, *Pantheon*, xvii (1936), p. 184. Montreal, Mus.
*Le wagon de troisième classe (c. 1862). 26¾ × 36¼. S. Ottawa, N.G.C.

EDGAR DEGAS, 1834–1917

Après le bain (c. 1900). Pastel, 24½ × 21½. S. Ref.: Lemoisne, *Degas* (1946), No. 1382. Toronto, Samuel Zacks.
*Au café-concert (c. 1884). P., 25½ × 18. Montreal, Samuel Bronfman.
Buste de femme (c. 1884). 17½ × 14. S. Ref.: Lemoisne, No. 804. Montreal, Lazarus Phillips.
*Chevaux de courses (1883–5). Pastel, 15 × 22. Ottawa, N.G.C.
*Danseuse rose (c. 1878). Pastel, 29½ × 16½. Toronto, Wilmot L. Matthews.
Danseuses (c. 1891). Pastel, 19½ × 12¾. Ref.: Lemoisne, No. 1103. Ottawa, N.G.C.
Danseuses (c. 1896–9). Pastel, 16¼ × 13. S. Winnipeg, J. A. MacAulay.
Danseuses à la barre (1884–8). Pastel, 43¼ × 37. Ref.: Lemoisne, No. 808. Ottawa, N.G.C.
Deux danseuses. Pastel, 23¼ × 19. Toronto, David Meltzer.
Femme au bain (c. 1892). 28 × 35. Ref.: Lemoisne, No. 1119. Toronto, A.G.
Portrait de jeune fille (c. 1888). 25½ × 17¾. Ref.: Lemoisne, No. 53. Toronto, R. W. Finlayson.
Trois danseuses, jupes violettes (c. 1898). Pastel, 29 × 19. S. Ref.: Lemoisne, No. 1339. Montreal, Lazarus Phillips.

EUGÈNE DELACROIX, 1798–1863

Lady Macbeth (1850). 16 × 12¾. S. Ref.: Robaut, No. 1171. Montreal, Mrs Howard W. Pillow.
Lionne et lion dans leur antre (1856). 15 × 18. S. Ref.: Robaut, No. 1308. Montreal, Mus.

La Montée au Calvaire (after Tiepolo). 19¼ × 18. S. Ref.: Tietze, *Pantheon*, xvii (1936), p. 185. Toronto, A.G.
Samson et Dalila. P., 8 × 10. Montreal, Mrs William Van Horne.

ANDRÉ DERAIN, 1880–1954

Dans la forêt (c. 1912). 21⅞ × 25¼. S. Ref.: Sutton, *Derain* (1959), p. 150, Pl. 30. Toronto, David Meltzer.
Fleurs. 12 × 11. S. Winnipeg, R. A. Purves.
Fleurs dans un panier. 22½ × 22½. S. Toronto, A.G.
Fleurs dans une vase (c. 1920). 32 × 25¾. Winnipeg, W. A. Murphy.
Head of a Boy (c. 1933). 16 × 15. S. Montreal, Lazarus Phillips.
Head of a Girl. 13½ × 10½. Montreal, Dr G. R. McCall.
Landscape (c. 1909–11). 25½ × 21¼. S. Toronto, Samuel Zacks.
Landscape with Bridge (1906). 13 × 16⅛. S. Montreal, Lazarus Phillips.
Landscape with Three Trees, L'Estaque (1906). 38 × 30½. S. Ref.: Leymarie, *Fauvism* (1959), reprod. in colour, p. 113. Toronto, Samuel Zacks.
Le Mur rose. 20¼ × 24¾. S. Ref.: *Studio*, cxii (1936), reprod. in colour, p. 57. Montreal, Mus.
Nature morte. 7 × 17½. S. Saskatoon, Frederick Mendel.
Nature morte (c. 1912). 37¼ × 26¼. S. Ottawa, N.G.C.
Nature morte (1924). 29 × 36. S. Toronto, Samuel Zacks.
Nude (1922–3). 25½ × 21¼. S. Hamilton, Herman Levy.
Paysage. W., 15 × 21. S. Montreal, S. Muhlstock.
Paysage au bord de la mer: la Côte d'Azur près Agay (1905). 21 × 25. S. Ref.: Duthuit, *Fauves* (1949), reprod. p. 32. Ottawa, N.G.C.
Portrait de femme (1918). 28 × 12¾. Toronto, Dr Irving Wayne.
Sous-bois (1920). 14½ × 15⅝. S. Vancouver, Mrs J. P. Fell.
Still Life. 9½ × 14. Montreal, Mus.
Still Life: Jug and Fruit. 12½ × 15½. S. Toronto, Dr William Landmann.
*Tower Bridge, London (1907). 26¼ × 39½. Winnipeg, J. A. MacAulay.

KEES VAN DONGEN, 1877–

Chevaux dans la rue Lépic. 29½ × 61. S. Saskatoon, Frederick Mendel.
Russian Doll and Plant. 21½ × 18. S. Montreal, Samuel Bronfman.

RAOUL DUFY, 1877–1953

Avila. 19½ × 25½. W.S. Montreal, Mus.
Beach at the Casino Marie-Christiane, Saint-Adresse (1902). 21¼ × 25½. S.D. Winnipeg, Dr A. C. Abbott.
Carnaval de Nice. 13½ × 17½. S. Winnipeg, R. G. B. Dickson.
Changing of the Guard. 16½ × 14. S. Saskatoon, Frederick Mendel.

La Console jaune au violon (1949). $39\frac{1}{2} \times 31\frac{1}{2}$. S. Ref.: Courthion, reprod. in colour, Pl. 144. Toronto, Samuel Zacks.

Église à Honfleur (c. 1904). $21\frac{3}{4} \times 18\frac{1}{4}$. S. Montreal, Maxwell Cummings.

Harbour Scene (c. 1907). 21×25. S. Toronto, Samuel Zacks.

Hommage à Mozart (1915). $31\frac{1}{2} \times 25\frac{3}{4}$. S. Ref.: Courthion, Dufy (1951), Pl. 55. Toronto, Samuel Zacks.

La Jetée à Trouville (1933). $18 \times 43\frac{1}{2}$. S.D. Winnipeg, A.G.

Léda (1936). G., $25 \times 19\frac{1}{4}$. S. Winnipeg, P. D. Curry.

Le Havre (1908). $21\frac{3}{4} \times 18\frac{1}{4}$. S. Saskatoon, Frederick Mendel.

Jardin de Caldas de Montbuy: gris (1949). $13 \times 16\frac{1}{4}$. S. Toronto, John David Eaton.

Jardin de Caldas de Montbuy: soleil (1949). $13\frac{1}{4} \times 16\frac{1}{4}$. S. Toronto, John David Eaton.

La Loire (1937). W., $19\frac{3}{8} \times 25\frac{3}{8}$. S.D. Toronto, Mrs A. C. Matthews.

Marine. $12\frac{3}{4} \times 15\frac{3}{4}$. London, Ont., S. E. Weir.

Les Moissons à Langres. W., $19\frac{3}{4} \times 25\frac{3}{4}$. S. Winnipeg, J. A. MacAulay.

Mosquée à Marrakesch (c. 1926). W., $19\frac{1}{2} \times 26$. S. Toronto, Samuel Zacks.

Orchestre (1951). P., 16×24. S. Montreal, Lazarus Phillips.

Le Palais du Sultan à Marrakesch (1926). W., 19×25. S. Ottawa, N.G.C.

La Place d'Hyères. $18\frac{1}{2} \times 21\frac{3}{4}$. S. Toronto, John David Eaton.

Les Pêcheurs (1907). $25\frac{1}{2} \times 32$. S. Ref.: Courthion, Pl. 59. Montreal, Mrs I. A. Chipman.

La Plage de Deauville (1930). $25\frac{3}{4} \times 32$. S. Saskatoon, Frederick Mendel.

*Le Port du Havre (c. 1905–6). $24 \times 28\frac{3}{4}$. S. Ref.: Leymarie, Fauvism (1959), reprod. in colour, p. 63. Toronto, A.G.

Race-track. W., 19×25. Montreal, Dr G. R. McCall.

Regatta at Henley (1927). $25\frac{1}{4} \times 32$. S. Toronto, David Meltzer.

Regatta. W., $17\frac{3}{4} \times 23$. S. Winnipeg, R. A. Purves.

Saint-Adresse (1906). $17\frac{5}{8} \times 20\frac{3}{4}$. S. Ref.: Cogniat, Dufy (1950), reprod. p. 1. Toronto, W. Landauer.

Saint-Paul de Vence (1920). $21\frac{3}{4} \times 18\frac{1}{4}$. S.D. Toronto, Samuel Zacks.

Vence (1920). $25\frac{3}{4} \times 31\frac{3}{4}$. S.D. Ottawa, N.G.C.

Venice (1938). W., $19\frac{1}{2} \times 25\frac{1}{4}$. S.D. Toronto, Mrs A. C. Matthews.

View from a Balcony (c. 1921). $25\frac{3}{4} \times 32$. S. Saskatoon, Frederick Mendel.

Village Square. W., $19\frac{1}{2} \times 25\frac{1}{2}$. S. Toronto, Samuel Zacks.

MAX ERNST, 1891–

Dormeuse (1955). $21\frac{1}{2} \times 18$. S. Saskatoon, Frederick Mendel.

HENRI FANTIN-LATOUR, 1836–1904

Adoration (c. 1875). $26 \times 32\frac{1}{2}$. Toronto, A.G.

Asters (1894). $21\frac{1}{2} \times 24\frac{1}{2}$. S.D. Montreal, Mrs Howard W. Pillow.

Bathing. $21\frac{1}{2} \times 25\frac{1}{2}$. Toronto, A.G.

Bouquet de jonquilles dans une vase en verre (1880). 16×13. S.D. Toronto, Mrs Melville Watson.

Bouquet de roses (1885). $14\frac{3}{4} \times 17\frac{3}{4}$. S.D. Ottawa, N.G.C.

Delphiniums (1887). 21×18. S.D. Ref.: Fantin-Latour, No. 1304. Montreal, Bernard Lande.

Dahlias (1875). $19\frac{3}{4} \times 18\frac{3}{4}$. S.D. Winnipeg, J. A. MacAulay.

The Dance. 21×32. S. Toronto, A.G.

*Féerie (1863). $38\frac{1}{2} \times 51\frac{1}{4}$. Montreal, Mus.

Fleurs (1862). $18 \times 15\frac{1}{2}$. S.D. Toronto, W. E. Phillips.

Fleurs d'automne (1864). 21×17. S.D. Ref.: Fantin-Latour, No. 246.

Fleurs (1882). 21×25. S.D. Ottawa, John Matthews.

*Fleurs de cerisiers (1872). $15\frac{3}{4} \times 13$. Winnipeg, J. A. MacAulay.

Fleurs et fruits (1878). $12\frac{1}{4} \times 9\frac{3}{4}$. S.D. Montreal, Mrs Howard W. Pillow.

Interior with Three Figures. $23\frac{1}{4} \times 28\frac{3}{4}$. S. Toronto, A.G.

Jeune femme (1873). $15\frac{1}{2} \times 12\frac{1}{2}$. S. Montreal, Mrs I. A. Chipman.

Nymph in the Forest. $14 \times 11\frac{3}{4}$. Toronto, A.G.

Les Pivoines (1876). $19\frac{5}{8} \times 17\frac{1}{4}$. S.D. Ref.: Fantin-Latour, No. 784. Montreal, Miss Olive Hosmer.

*Portrait du jeune Fitz-James (1867). $20\frac{1}{2} \times 16\frac{3}{4}$. Hamilton, A.G. (stolen 1960).

Readers. 7×7. Montreal, Mus.

Reclining: Night Scene. $8\frac{1}{2} \times 17\frac{3}{4}$. Toronto, A.G.

Roses (1885). $17\frac{1}{2} \times 21\frac{1}{2}$. S.D. Ottawa, N.G.C.

Roses Gloire de Dijon (1891). $12\frac{3}{4} \times 15\frac{1}{4}$. S.D. Winnipeg, R. A. Purves.

Roses, Peaches, and Plums (1878). $12 \times 21\frac{1}{4}$. S.D. Ref.: Fantin-Latour, No. 896 or 902. Toronto, A.G.

Still Life: Fruit (1870). $13\frac{1}{4} \times 10\frac{7}{8}$. S.D. Ref.: Fantin-Latour, No. 444. Montreal, Mrs Howard W. Pillow.

Still Life: Roses and Grapes (1876). 14×19. Ref.: Fantin-Latour, No. 792. Winnipeg, J. A. MacAulay.

Temptation of St Anthony (c. 1893). $8\frac{1}{4} \times 18\frac{1}{4}$. Toronto, A.G.

La Toilette. $11\frac{3}{4} \times 10\frac{1}{2}$. S. Montreal, Dr A. T. Henderson.

JEAN-LOUIS FORAIN, 1852–1931

Au Piano. P., $7\frac{7}{8} \times 10\frac{1}{8}$. S. Vancouver, Mrs J. P. Fell.

L'Avocat (1907). $21\frac{1}{4} \times 25\frac{3}{4}$. S. D. Ottawa, N.G.C.

PAUL GAUGUIN, 1848–1903

Apples. $14\frac{1}{2} \times 6\frac{3}{4}$. Winnipeg, J. A. MacAulay.

Jeune garçon (1888). $11\frac{1}{4} \times 8\frac{1}{2}$. D. Ottawa, G. H. Southam.

Nature morte. 13×16. Ottawa, N.G.C.

*Paysage à Pont-Aven (1885–7). $23\frac{1}{2} \times 28\frac{1}{2}$. Ottawa, N.G.C.

Paysage à Pont-Aven (1888). $30 \times 24\frac{1}{2}$. S.D. St Andrews East, Que., Mrs L. T. Porter.

Vase de fleurs (1884–5). $12\frac{1}{2} \times 18$. S. Montreal, Lazarus Phillips.

ALBERT GLEIZES, 1881–1953

Le Port (1912). $35\frac{1}{2} \times 45\frac{7}{8}$. S.D. Toronto, A.G.

VINCENT VAN GOGH, 1853–1890

Les Chardons (1889). $15\frac{3}{4} \times 12\frac{3}{4}$. Ref.: De la Faille, *Van Gogh* (1928), No. 599. Winnipeg, J. A. MacAulay.

Chaumière de Brabant (1885). $12\frac{1}{2} \times 16$. Ref.: De la Faille, No. 89. Winnipeg, J. A. MacAulay.

Farm near Drenthe (*c.* 1883). $7 \times 12\frac{1}{4}$. Winnipeg, J. A. MacAulay.

*Iris (1888–9). Oil on paper, $24\frac{1}{2} \times 19$. Ottawa, N.G.C.

Nature morte (*c.* 1885). $12 \times 18\frac{1}{2}$. Ref.: De la Faille, No. 336. Toronto, Mrs E. E. Johnson.

Nature morte: Fleurs (1886–8). 25×18. S. Ref.: De la Faille, No. 241. Ottawa, N.G.C.

*Nature morte: Fleurs (*c.* 1887). $19\frac{1}{2} \times 24$. Ottawa, N.G.C.

Paysanne de Nuenen pelant des pommes de terre (1885). P., $16\frac{1}{2} \times 12\frac{1}{4}$. Ref.: De la Faille, No. 145. Winnipeg, E. S. Cooper.

Peasant Woman Walking through the Fields (1889). 18×15. Ref.: De la Faille, *Van Gogh* (1939), No. 715. Montreal, Lazarus Phillips.

Tête de paysanne (1885). $15\frac{1}{2} \times 11\frac{1}{4}$. Ref.: De la Faille, No. 144. Montreal, Miss Olive Hosmer.

*Tête de paysanne de Brabant (1885). $15\frac{3}{4} \times 13\frac{1}{4}$. S. Ref.: De la Faille, No. 141. Winnipeg, J. A. MacAulay.

MARCEL GROMAIRE, 1892–

Nude (1927). $10\frac{3}{4} \times 8\frac{3}{4}$. S.D. Toronto, Samuel Zacks.

JUAN GRIS, 1887–1927

Harlequin et pierrot (1924). $16 \times 10\frac{3}{4}$. S.D. Toronto, Samuel Zacks.

Nature morte à la clarinette (1912–21). $18\frac{1}{2} \times 24\frac{1}{2}$. S.D. Ref.: Kahnweiler, *Gris* (1947), Pl. 71. Toronto, Samuel Zacks.

Nature morte à la pipe (1918). 14×9. S. Toronto, Samuel Zacks.

JEAN-BAPTISTE-ARMAND GUILLAUMIN, 1841–1927

Environs de Crozant. $19\frac{1}{2} \times 23\frac{1}{2}$. London, Ont., S.E. Weir.

Le Trayas (1907). 25×31. S.D. Toronto, Samuel Zacks.

HENRI HARPIGNIES, 1819–1916

La Côte d'Azur. $20\frac{1}{4} \times 14\frac{1}{4}$. S. Winnipeg, R. G. B. Dickson.

Landscape. $37 \times 50\frac{1}{2}$. Hamilton, A.G.

Mediterranean Landscape (1865). $39\frac{1}{4} \times 49\frac{1}{2}$. S.D. Montreal, Mus.

A Summer Day (1890). 15×22. S.D. Montreal, Mus.

JEAN-AUGUSTE-DOMINIQUE INGRES, 1780–1867

Study for 'The Iliad' in *The Apotheosis of Homer* (attr.) (*c.* 1827). $25 \times 31\frac{1}{2}$. Toronto, A.G.

ROGER DE LA FRESNAYE, 1885–1925

Cimitière (1909). $19\frac{1}{2} \times 26$. S.D. Toronto, Samuel Zacks.

MARIE LAURENCIN, 1885–1956

Andromède (1928). $21\frac{1}{8} \times 17\frac{3}{8}$. S.D. Toronto, Gerald Larkin.

Concert. $22 \times 18\frac{1}{2}$. S. Vancouver, Thomas Ingledow.

Head of a Girl (1918). Oil on paper. $20\frac{1}{2} \times 17\frac{1}{2}$. S. Toronto, David Meltzer.

Jeune fille (1928). 18×22. S.D. Toronto, Gerald Larkin.

Portrait of a Woman. $13\frac{3}{4} \times 10\frac{3}{4}$. S. Toronto, W. Landauer.

Three Figures (1923). 35×39. S.D. Toronto, John David Eaton.

Portrait de Mme B (1905). W., $7\frac{1}{2} \times 4\frac{3}{4}$. S.D. Toronto, Samuel Zacks.

Two Girls. W., $17\frac{1}{4} \times 13\frac{1}{2}$. S. Montreal, Lazarus Phillips.

FERNAND LÉGER, 1881–1955

Ajaccio (1907). $23\frac{1}{2} \times 42\frac{1}{2}$. Montreal, Mrs I. A. Chipman.

Femme au compotier (1924). $29 \times 36\frac{1}{2}$, S.D. Toronto, David Meltzer.

Les Plongeuses: study (1940). G., $22\frac{1}{2} \times 16$. Montreal, Dr Jules Brahy.

Les Plongeuses: study (1941). G., $21\frac{1}{2} \times 15\frac{1}{2}$. Toronto, A.G.

*Still Life (1919). $47 \times 34\frac{1}{2}$. Toronto, Samuel Zacks.

The Two Knives (1949). 19×25. S.D. Toronto, Dr William Landmann.

ÉDOUARD MANET, 1832–1883

Femme au nœud bleu. Pastel on canvas, $22 \times 18\frac{1}{2}$. Ref.: Jamot and Wildenstein, *Manet* (1932), No. 349. Montreal, Lazarus Phillips.

Portrait de femme. Pastel on canvas, $20\frac{3}{4} \times 17\frac{1}{2}$. S. Ref.: Jamot and Wildenstein, No. 355. Montreal, Mus.

ALBERT MARQUET, 1875–1947

Paysage du Midi (1908). $16\frac{1}{2} \times 13\frac{1}{2}$. S. Montreal, Lazarus Phillips.

La petite place au réverbère (*c.* 1904). $24\frac{3}{4} \times 28\frac{3}{4}$. S. Ottawa, N.G.C.

Le Phare à Saint-Tropez (*c.* 1935). $8\frac{3}{4} \times 10\frac{3}{4}$. S. Toronto, Samuel Zacks.

Le Pont Marie (*c.* 1911). $25\frac{1}{2} \times 32$. S. Hamilton, A.G.

Le Pont Neuf. $25 \times 31\frac{1}{2}$. S. Toronto, Samuel Zacks.

*L'Usine au bord du canal (1909). $25\frac{1}{4} \times 31\frac{1}{4}$. Hamilton, Herman Levy.

Vue de la Seine (*c.* 1911). $25\frac{1}{2} \times 32$. S. Montreal, Lazarus Phillips.

ANDRÉ MASSON, 1896–

Picking Figs. Pastel, 25¼ × 19¼. Toronto, Samuel Zacks.

Spectre d'hiver. 21½ × 18. S. Edmonton, H. A. Dyde.

HENRI MATISSE, 1869–1954

★Femme à la fenêtre au bord de la mer (1922). 28½ × 36½. Montreal, Mus.

Girl in Rose Dress (1942). 21½ × 12¾. S.D. Toronto, Samuel Zacks.

Ivy Branch (1941). 21¾ × 18. S.D. Toronto, Samuel Zacks.

Jeune femme à la toque persane (c. 1916). P., 21½ × 14¾. S. Toronto, Samuel Zacks.

Nature morte au purro, I (1904). 23⅝ × 28¼. S. Ref.: Barr, p. 59, reprod. p. 314. Montreal, Lazarus Phillips.

★Nu au canapé jaune (1926). 21¼ × 32. Ottawa, N.G.C.

Odalisque au miroir (c. 1924). 15¼ × 13. S. Toronto, Samuel Zacks.

Pastorale: study (c. 1905). 16 × 12½. S. Montreal, Lazarus Phillips.

Sylvie la danseuse (1924). 22 × 18. S. Ref.: Cahiers d'Art, No. 7 (1926), reprod. p. 56. Toronto, David Meltzer.

JEAN-FRANÇOIS MILLET, 1814–1875

Man with a Hoe. P., 18⅛ × 14⅞. Montreal, P. F. Osler.

★Œdipe détaché de l'arbre (1847). 52½ × 20½. S. Ottawa, N.G.C.

Portrait de Mme Millet. 13¼ × 10½. S. Montreal, Miss Olive Hosmer.

Smithy, Normandy. 10 × 12. Montreal, Mrs William Van Horne.

Young Woman Churning (c. 1849). 11½ × 6½. S. Montreal, Mus.

JOAN MIRÓ, 1893–

Femme et oiseau devant le soleil. 13¾ × 10½. Winnipeg, P. D. Curry.

Painting, Summer 1936. B., 30¾ × 42½. S. Toronto, Samuel Zacks.

Women, Birds, Stars (1942). W. and pastel, 19½ × 25½. Toronto, Samuel Zacks.

CLAUDE MONET, 1840–1926

Étretat: l'Aiguille et la Roche Percée (c. 1885). P., 32 × 15¼. S.D. Montreal, Murray Vaughan.

Les Falaises de Pourville (1886). 25¾ × 39½. Montreal, P. F. Osler.

Les Falaises de Pourville (1897). 25½ × 40. S.D. Montreal, Mus.

Falaise près de Fécamp (1881). 23¼ × 30¾. S.D. Montreal, P. F. Osler.

Falaise près de Pourville (1882). 23¼ × 28½. S.D. Ref.: Reuterswärd, Monet (1948), p. 284. Montreal, Maxwell Cummings.

★Le Jardin de l'artiste à Giverny (1881). 39½ × 32. Ref.: Malingue, Monet (1943), Pl. 113. Montreal, Oskar Federer.

Landscape on the Epte at Giverny (1885). 30 × 38. S. Montreal, Samuel Bronfman.

Mer agitée (c. 1884). 23⅝ × 29. S. Ref.: Reuterswärd, p. 281. Ottawa, N.G.C.

The Normandy Coast near Villerville (1867). 20½ × 24½. Montreal, Mrs William Van Horne.

Les Nymphéas. 52 × 38. S. Montreal, Bernard Lande.

Les Nymphéas (1907). 38¾ × 39. Toronto, E. B. Kernaghan.

★Les Rochers de Pourville (1882). 25¾ × 32. S.D. Montreal, Lazarus Phillips.

Seascape with Cliffs and Sailing Boats (1882). 23½ × 31. S.D. Winnipeg, J. A. MacAulay.

Vétheuil. 19¼ × 25. S. Winnipeg, R. A. Purves.

★Vétheuil en été (1879). 26¾ × 35⅝. S.D. Toronto, A.G.

★Waterloo Bridge (1903). 25½ × 39¼. S.D. Hamilton, Herman Levy.

Waterloo Bridge: le soleil dans le brouillard (1903). 27½ × 38½. S.D. Ref.: Reuterswärd, p. 287. Ottawa, N.G.C.

ADOLPHE MONTICELLI, 1824–1886

Adoration of the Magi. P., 14 × 26. S. Montreal, Mrs William Van Horne.

Bathing Pool. 15½ × 23. Vancouver, A.G.

The Conversion of St Paul. P., 7¾ × 15½. Montreal, Mrs William Van Horne.

Dancers in a Wood. P., 23½ × 15½. S. Montreal, Mrs William Van Horne.

Dancing Girls. 13¾ × 24. S. Ottawa, N.G.C.

The Decameron. P., 12½ × 20. Montreal, Mrs William Van Horne.

Don Quixote and Sancho Panza. P., 11¾ × 14¼. S. Ottawa, N.G.C.

Fête champêtre. 18 × 26. S. Montreal, Mus.

Fête champêtre. P., 13 × 25. S. Montreal, Mrs William Van Horne.

Fête champêtre: a Summer Idyll. 32 × 47. Montreal, R. F. Angus.

Fête intime. 13¾ × 20. S. Montreal, Mus.

Figures. 21½ × 40. S. Vancouver, Mrs J. T. Rogers.

Fleurs diverses. P., 19 × 14½. S. Winnipeg, J. A. MacAulay.

The Fountain. P., 10¾ × 7¾. S. Montreal, Mrs William Van Horne.

The Fountain of Youth. 15½ × 23½. S. Toronto, A.G.

Garden Fête. 9¾ × 22½. Toronto, A.G.

Garden Party. 12 × 24. S. Montreal, Mus.

Gate of a Fort. 15½ × 23½. S. Montreal, Mus.

Group of Figures. 17¼ × 12. Edmonton, E. E. Poole.

The Kitchen. P., circular, 9¾ diameter. Montreal, Mrs William Van Horne.

Mardi Gras. 9½ × 13½. Toronto, A.G.

Mountain Landscape near Algiers. P., 12¾ × 35. S. Montreal, Mrs William Van Horne.

The Promenade. P., 9⅞ × 8. Toronto, A.G.

Return from the Chase. P., 16½ × 27. S. Montreal, Mrs William Van Horne.

Return from the Chase. 25½ × 39½. S. Toronto, A.G.

A Southern Garden. 14 × 10¼. Montreal, Mrs William Van Horne.

A Walled Lane. P., 15¾ × 24. S. Montreal, Mrs William Van Horne.

BERTHE MORISOT, 1841–1895

*Fillette à la poupée (1883). 29 × 28. Montreal, Maxwell Cummings.

Seated Woman with Parasol. 36 × 28. S. Toronto, Mrs G. W. Robinette.

JULES PASCIN, 1885–1930

Reclining Woman. 28½ × 36. S. Toronto, Samuel Zacks.

Three Girls. G. on B., 14½ × 22¼. S. Toronto, Samuel Zacks.

FRANCIS PICABIA, 1879–1953

Road with Trees. 30 × 37. Saskatoon, Frederick Mendel.

PABLO PICASSO, 1881–

Buste de femme (1909). G. on B., 24⅞ × 19. S. Ref.: Zervos, *Picasso*, ii (i) (1942), Pl. 142. Montreal, Lazarus Phillips.

Compotier et tasse (1910). 15 × 21½. S. Ref.: Zervos, ii (i), Pl. 190. Toronto, David Meltzer.

Deux nus (1920). Mixed media on paper. 19 × 24¾. S. Ref.: Zervos, vi, No. 1404. Toronto, Samuel Zacks.

Égyptienne (1916). P., 12¾ × 8¾. S.D. Ref.: Zervos, ii (ii), Pl. 563, Toronto, Samuel Zacks.

*Femme assise (1903). 32 × 21¼. Ottawa, G. H. Southam.

Femme assise, fond bleu (c. 1950). P., 36½ × 29. S. Toronto, John David Eaton.

*Le Guéridon (1919). 45¾ × 28¾. Ottawa, N.G.C.

Nu aux mains serrés (1905). G. on canvas, 37¾ × 29¾. S.D. on back. Ref.: Zervos, i, No. 310. Toronto, Samuel Zacks.

L'Ombre de l'artiste sur la femme (1954). 38¼ × 51¼. S. Toronto, Samuel Zacks.

La Soupe (1902). 15 × 18. Toronto, D. M. Dunlap.

Still Life: Jug with Flowers. G., 12 × 9½. S. Winnipeg, J. A. MacAulay.

Woman Seated on a Chair (1900). Pastel, 14¾ × 19½. S. Ref.: Zervos, vi, No, 335. Winnipeg, J. A. MacAulay.

Woman with Necklace (1901). B., 17¼ × 14¼. S. Ref.: Zervos, vi, Pl. 385. Toronto, Samuel Zacks.

CAMILLE PISSARRO, 1830–1903

Bois de châtaigniers en hiver, Louveciennes (1872). 10½ × 16. S.D. Ref.: Pissarro and Venturi, *Pissarro* (1939), No. 144. Ottawa, Mrs J. D. Bogue.

Le Crête du Chou à Pontoise, printemps (1879). 18 × 22. S.D. Montreal, Lazarus Phillips.

*Dulwich College (1871). 19¾ × 23¾. Winnipeg, J. A. MacAulay.

Effet de neige, Bazincourt. P., 5½ × 8¾. Winnipeg, H. L. Thompson.

Éragny, été. P., 5½ × 8½. S. Winnipeg, H. L. Thompson.

Étude de paysan (Semeur à Montfoucault) (c. 1875). 25¾ × 21¼. S. Ref.: Pissarro and Venturi, No. 330. Montreal, Maxwell Cummings.

Femme cassant du bois (c. 1890). G., 23½ × 19. S. Ref.: Pissarro and Venturi, No. 1455. Toronto, Dr William Landmann.

Femme se coiffant (c. 1894). Pastel, 20½ × 17½. S. Ref.: Pissarro and Venturi, No. 1599. Ottawa, N.G.C.

Fenaison à Éragny (1901). 21¼ × 25½. Ref.: Pissarro and Venturi, No. 1207. Ottawa, N.G.C.

La Grange, matin, Éragny (1893). 18 × 21. S.D. Ref.: Pissarro and Venturi, No. 975. Montreal, Dr S. Graham Ross.

Paysage vert (c. 1875). 14½ × 17½. S. Winnipeg, J. A. MacAulay.

Peupliers, temps gris, Éragny (1895). 23 × 31. S.D. Ref.: Pissarro and Venturi, No. 740. Toronto, A.G.

Pommiers en fleurs (1870). 17¾ × 21¾. S.D. Ref.: Pissarro and Venturi, No. 84. Hamilton, Herman Levy.

*Le Pont Boieledieu à Rouen, temps mouillé (1896). 29 × 36. S. Ref.: Pissarro and Venturi, No. 948. Toronto, A.G.

Le Pont de pierre et les Péniches à Rouen (1883). 21 × 25. S.D. Ref.: Pissarro and Venturi, No. 605. Toronto, A.G.

Le Pont de Pierre à Rouen, temps gris (1896). 26 × 36. S.D. Ref.: Pissarro and Venturi, No. 963. Ottawa, N.G.C.

Le Port de Rouen (1898). 25½ × 31½. S.D. Ref.: Pissarro and Venturi, No. 1054. Montreal, Mus.

Printemps, temps gris, Éragny (1895). 23½ × 28. S.D. Ref.: Pissarro and Venturi, No. 743. Toronto, A.G.

Printemps, temps gris, Éragny (1895). 23¾ × 28¾. S.D. Ref.: Pissarro and Venturi, No. 912. Toronto, A.G.

Le Quai de Pothius, Pontoise (1872). 18 × 22. S.D. Ref.: Pissarro and Venturi, No. 189. Montreal, U. L. Steiner.

*Rue à L'Hermitage à Pontoise (1875). 23 × 36. Ottawa, N.G.C.

Rue Saint-Lazare (1897). 14 × 11. S.D. Ref.: Pissarro and Venturi, No. 985. Saskatoon, Frederick Mendel.

Le Sentier de Bazincourt (1884). 21¼ × 25½. S.D. Ref.: Pissarro and Venturi, No. 637. Toronto, John David Eaton.

L'Usine à Pontoise (1873). 15 × 22. S.D. Ref.: Pissarro and Venturi, No. 217. Montreal, Samuel Bronfman.

PIERRE PUVIS DE CHAVANNES, 1824–1898

Les Bienfaits de la paix (c. 1890). 25½ × 67½. Ottawa, N.G.C.

ODILON REDON, 1840–1916

Bouquet de fleurs des champs. 21¾ × 15. S. Winnipeg, J. A. MacAulay.

Buste d'enfant. Pastel, 17½ × 11¾. Montreal, Gerald Bronfman.

Fleurs. 21¼ × 18. S. Montreal, Samuel Bronfman.

Fleurs exotiques. Pastel, $24\frac{5}{8} \times 19\frac{3}{8}$. S. Ottawa, N.G.C.
Vase de fleurs. Pastel, $27\frac{1}{2} \times 21$. S. Montreal, Lazarus Phillips.
*Vase de fleurs (*c.* 1915). $24\frac{1}{2} \times 21\frac{1}{2}$. Toronto, A.G.
Le Vitrail: Head with Flowers. $25\frac{1}{4} \times 21\frac{3}{4}$. S. Ref.: Fegdal, *Redon* (1929), Pl. xlix. Montreal, Lazarus Phillips.

PIERRE-AUGUSTE RENOIR, 1841–1919

Bowl and Oranges. $5\frac{1}{2} \times 10\frac{1}{4}$. S. Montreal, Mrs Howard W. Pillow.
Buste de femme nue (1888–90). $21\frac{5}{8} \times 18\frac{1}{8}$. S. Ref.: Drucker, *Renoir* (1944), reprod. in colour, Pl. 98. Winnipeg, J. A. MacAulay.
Buste de fillette (1895). $16\frac{1}{2} \times 13$. S. Winnipeg, R. A. Purves.
Cagnes (*c.* 1910). $8 \times 10\frac{1}{4}$. Winnipeg, J. A. MacAulay.
*Claude et Renée (1903). 31×25. Ottawa, N.G.C.
Le Concert (1919). $29\frac{3}{4} \times 36\frac{1}{2}$. Ref.: Drucker, *Renoir* (1955), Pl. 142. Toronto, A.G.
Cup and Saucer. $6 \times 8\frac{1}{4}$. S. Montreal, Murray Vaughan.
Deux filles à la plage. $14\frac{3}{4} \times 13\frac{1}{4}$. S. Ref.: Vollard, *Renoir* (1918), ii, Pl. 95. Winnipeg, J. A. MacAulay.
Entrée de la propriété du Général d'Oisel. $25\frac{3}{4} \times 20$. S. Montreal, Mus.
Les Environs de Toulon. 18×21. S. Toronto, Mrs G. W. Robinette.
Esquisse de paysage (1902). $10\frac{1}{4} \times 13\frac{1}{4}$. S. Vancouver, Mrs J. P. Fell.
Gabrielle (1905). $11\frac{1}{4} \times 10\frac{3}{4}$. S. Montreal, Lazarus Phillips.
Jeune fille au chapeau. $16 \times 12\frac{1}{2}$. S. Montreal, Dr A. T. Henderson.
Paysage. 16×13. S. Saskatoon, Frederick Mendel.
Paysage à Cannes (1908). $11\frac{1}{2} \times 12\frac{3}{4}$. S. Vancouver, Mrs J. P. Fell.
Petite rivière. $11\frac{1}{4} \times 16\frac{1}{2}$. S. Montreal, Guy Drummond.
Portrait de Claude (*c.* 1903). $16 \times 12\frac{1}{2}$. S. Ref.: *Atelier de Renoir* (1931), i, No. 271. Toronto, A.G.
Portrait de jeune fille. 16×12. S. Ref.: Vollard, ii, Pl. 94. Winnipeg, J. A. MacAulay.
Portrait de Mme X (1875). $25\frac{3}{4} \times 21\frac{1}{2}$. S. Montreal, Samuel Bronfman.
Réunion autour d'un bâteau (1862). $19\frac{1}{2} \times 23\frac{1}{2}$. S.D. Ref.: Vollard, i, Pl. 8, No. 30. Montreal, Maxwell Cummings.
Roses in a Bowl. $20\frac{1}{4} \times 18$. S. Montreal, Mrs Howard W. Pillow.
Rue de village. 9×16. S. Winnipeg, R. A. Purves.
La Seine à Chatou (*c.* 1871). 18×22. S. Ref.: Leclerc, *Renoir* (1948), reprod. p. 9. Toronto, A.G.
Sous-bois (1865–6). $28\frac{1}{2} \times 23\frac{1}{4}$. Montreal, Oskar Federer.
Sucrier, verre et citron. $12\frac{7}{8} \times 14\frac{3}{4}$. S. Winnipeg, J. A. MacAulay.
Ten Studies (1888). 18×15. Montreal, Lazarus Phillips.
*Tête de napolitaine. 14×12. Montreal, Mus.
Washerwomen in a Landscape. 18×21. S. Toronto, Mrs G. W. Robinette.

GEORGES ROUAULT, 1871–1958

Le Chirurgien. G., $18 \times 11\frac{1}{8}$. Ref.: *Canadian Art*, xii (1954), reprod. p. 32. Toronto, A.G. (stolen 1954).
Crucifixion. $29 \times 22\frac{1}{4}$. S. Ottawa, G. H. Southam.
Crucifixion. $30\frac{1}{2} \times 23\frac{1}{2}$. S. Montreal, Mus.
L'Écuyère. $21\frac{1}{2} \times 18$. S. Montreal, Mrs I. A. Chipman.
La Face. 12×15. Saskatoon, Frederick Mendel.
Figure de cirque (*c.* 1935). G., $28 \times 19\frac{1}{2}$. Toronto, T. M. Sterling.
Filles de cirque (*c.* 1935). B., $20\frac{1}{2} \times 25\frac{1}{4}$. S. Toronto, Samuel Zacks.
Flowers (1923). $20\frac{1}{2} \times 16$. Toronto, David Meltzer.
L'Homme à la pipe (*c.* 1935). $15\frac{3}{4} \times 13$. Toronto, John David Eaton.
Monique (*c.* 1932). Oil on paper, $20\frac{3}{8} \times 14\frac{1}{2}$. S. Toronto, T. M. Sterling.
Nature morte (1937). $22\frac{1}{2} \times 15\frac{3}{4}$. S. Toronto, Samuel Zacks.
*Pierrette. $30\frac{1}{4} \times 22\frac{1}{4}$. Montreal, Dr G. R. McCall.
Profil de femme (*c.* 1935). $18\frac{1}{4} \times 13\frac{1}{4}$. S. Toronto, Samuel Zacks.
Profil de femme. $25 \times 18\frac{1}{2}$. S. Toronto, John David Eaton.
Three Miners (1930). G., 13×11. Montreal, Lazarus Phillips.
Two Clowns. G., $7\frac{1}{2} \times 9\frac{3}{4}$. S. Winnipeg, J. A. MacAulay.
Two Clowns. G., $7\frac{1}{2} \times 9\frac{3}{4}$. S. Winnipeg, J. A. MacAulay.

THÉODORE ROUSSEAU, 1812–1867

The Brook: Autumn Landscape. $12\frac{1}{2} \times 21\frac{1}{2}$. S. Montreal, Mrs William Van Horne.
Church in a Valley. $8\frac{1}{4} \times 13\frac{1}{2}$. S. Ottawa, N.G.C.
Crossing the Brook. $25 \times 16\frac{1}{2}$. Toronto, A.G.
Fallen Tree. Montreal, S. Muhlstock.
Forest Interior. $16\frac{3}{4} \times 22\frac{1}{2}$. Ottawa, N.G.C.
The Great Oaks of Bas-Breau, Forest of Fontainebleau. 35×46. Montreal, Mrs William Van Horne.
Landscape with Larches. $16\frac{1}{2} \times 15\frac{1}{4}$. Montreal, Mrs William Van Horne.
The Pond. P., $9\frac{1}{2} \times 7\frac{1}{2}$. Ottawa, N.G.C.
Sunset. $6 \times 8\frac{1}{2}$. Montreal, Mus.
Thatched Cottages. B., 8×11. Montreal, Mrs William Van Horne.

ANDRÉ DUNOYER DE SEGONZAC, 1884–

River Landscape. W., 26×20. S. Toronto, A.G.
Trees. W., 18×12. S. Montreal, Oskar Federer.

PAUL SÉRUSIER, 1863–1927

Nature morte (1921). $28\frac{1}{4} \times 19\frac{1}{4}$. S.D. Montreal, Maxwell Cummings.
Paysage à Pont-Aven (1890). $25\frac{3}{4} \times 32$. S.D. Ottawa, N.G.C.

PAUL SIGNAC, 1863–1935

Le Petit Andeley. W., $10\frac{1}{4} \times 16$. S. Montreal, Oskar Federer.

ALFRED SISLEY, 1839–1899

Bordes de l'Oise—automne (1873). $18\frac{1}{4} \times 24\frac{1}{4}$. S.D. Ref.: Daulte, *Sisley* (1959), No. 94. Montreal, Mus.

Chemin de By au Bois des Roches—Courant—été de Saint-Martin (1881). $23 \times 31\frac{1}{2}$. S. Ref.: Daulte, No. 433. Montreal, Mus.

★Les Côteaux de Bougival (1875). $19\frac{3}{4} \times 23\frac{1}{2}$. S.D. Ottawa, N.G.C.

Environs de Moret-sur-Loing (1890). $18\frac{1}{4} \times 21\frac{3}{4}$. S.D. Ref.: Daulte, No. 728. Winnipeg, J. A. MacAulay.

La Falaise de Penarth, le soir—temps orag eux (1897). $21\frac{1}{2} \times 25\frac{3}{4}$. S.D. Ref.: Daulte, No. 867. Fredericton, Beaverbrook A.G.

Farmhouse (1876). $15\frac{7}{8} \times 24$. Halifax, Prince John Loewenstein.

Garage de bâteaux à Saint-Mammes. $21 \times 28\frac{1}{2}$. S. Montreal, P. F. Osler.

Landscape with House (1887). $21 \times 28\frac{1}{2}$. S.D. Winnipeg, R. A. Purves.

Laveuses près de Champagne (1882). $19\frac{1}{4} \times 28\frac{1}{2}$. S. Ref.: Daulte, No. 466. Ottawa, N.G.C.

Neige de mars et dégel. Pastel, $12 \times 15\frac{3}{4}$. S. Montreal, Guy Drummond.

L'Oise à Marly (1885). $21 \times 28\frac{1}{2}$. S.D. Toronto, D. M. Dunlap.

Paysage près de Moret (1884). $21\frac{3}{8} \times 28\frac{7}{8}$. Ref.: Daulte, No. 542. Toronto, A.G.

Une rue à Louveciennes (1875). 15×21. S. Ref.: Daulte, No. 167. Montreal, Lazarus Phillips.

Saint-Mammes—temps gris (1884). $18 \times 21\frac{1}{2}$. S. Ref.: Daulte, No. 506. Toronto, A.G.

CHAIM SOUTINE, 1894–1943

L'Église du village (c. 1920). $23\frac{1}{2} \times 31$. Toronto, Samuel Zacks.

HENRI DE TOULOUSE-LAUTREC, 1864–1901

Study for the Poster 'Babylone d'Allemagne'. Oil on paper, 23×15. Montreal, Lazarus Phillips.

CONSTANT TROYON, 1810–1865

Le Guitariste: portrait de George Sand. 36×29. Montreal, Mrs William Van Horne.

Landscape with Figures and Cattle. P., 9×13. S. Toronto, A.G.

MAURICE UTRILLO, 1883–1955

Argenteuil, la cour de l'École (1925). 15×21. S.D. Winnipeg, W. A. Murphy.

L'Église de Châtillon. 13×16. Port Hope, Lionel Massey.

L'Église de Clichy (c. 1911). B., 24×20. Toronto, D. M. Dunlap.

L'Église de Domrémy (1924). $28\frac{1}{4} \times 36\frac{1}{4}$. S. Hamilton, Herman Levy.

L'Église de Groslay (1915). $19\frac{1}{2} \times 25\frac{1}{4}$. S. Saskatoon, Frederick Mendel.

L'Église de Monnerville (1928). $39\frac{3}{4} \times 29$. Vancouver, Walter Koerner.

Hôpital militaire Saint-Martin, à Paris. G., 19×25. S. Toronto, John David Eaton.

★La Maison de Berlioz et pavillon de chasse Henri IV (c. 1917). $21\frac{1}{4} \times 28\frac{3}{4}$. S. Ref.: Werner, *Utrillo* (1955), reprod. in colour, Pl. 24. Toronto, A.G.

La Porte de Compiègne. P., $22\frac{3}{4} \times 30\frac{1}{2}$. S. Montreal, Mus.

Rue Norvins à Montmartre (c. 1911). $28\frac{3}{4} \times 19\frac{3}{4}$. S. Ref.: Pétridès, *Utrillo*, i (1959), No. 224. Toronto, Samuel Zacks.

Rue Saint-Vincent à Montmartre. 15×18. S. Winnipeg, J. A. MacAulay.

Rue Saint-Rustique avec le café La Belle Gabrielle. B., $18 \times 21\frac{1}{2}$. S. Toronto, John David Eaton.

Still Life: Lily of the Valley. 18×14. Montreal, Murray Vaughan.

Street. $18 \times 21\frac{1}{2}$. S. Winnipeg, R. A. Purves.

Street in Montmartre. $18\frac{1}{4} \times 21\frac{3}{4}$. S. Winnipeg, R. A. Purves.

Street in Montmartre (1922). 9×12. S.D. Montreal, Mrs Howard W. Pillow.

SUZANNE VALADON, 1867–1938

Vase de fleurs (1920). 24×20. S.D. Montreal, Maxwell Cummings.

LOUIS VALTAT, 1869–1952

Au Cabaret du Lapin Agile (c. 1896). $31\frac{1}{2} \times 24\frac{1}{2}$. Toronto, Samuel Zacks.

JACQUES VILLON, 1875–

Les jeunes demoiselles (1930). $28 \times 22\frac{1}{2}$. S.D. Toronto, Vincent Tovell.

Louisette (1928). $32 \times 23\frac{1}{2}$. S.D. Toronto, Vincent Tovell.

Self-portrait (1936). 18×15. S.D. Toronto, Vincent Tovell.

La Moisson (1943). $24\frac{1}{4} \times 20$. S. Toronto, Samuel Zacks.

Self-portrait (1934). $21\frac{1}{2} \times 18$. S.D. Toronto, Vincent Tovell.

MAURICE DE VLAMINCK, 1876–1958

Apples and Pears (c. 1924). Oil on paper, $7\frac{1}{2} \times 33\frac{1}{2}$. S. Toronto, David Meltzer.

★Les Écluses à Bougival (1906). $21\frac{3}{8} \times 25\frac{1}{2}$. Ottawa, N.G.C.

Fleurs. $20\frac{1}{2} \times 15\frac{1}{4}$. Winnipeg, A.G.

Fleurs. $23\frac{3}{4} \times 19\frac{1}{2}$. S. Montreal, Mrs Howard W. Pillow.

Landscape (1909). $28\frac{3}{4} \times 36\frac{1}{4}$. S. Toronto, W. Landauer.

Landscape (c. 1917). $23\frac{1}{2} \times 31$. S. Toronto, Samuel Zacks.

Landscape (1920). $23\frac{1}{2} \times 28\frac{1}{2}$. S. Toronto, Dr Irving Wayne.

Landscape with Farm Buildings. $19\frac{3}{4} \times 24$. S. Montreal, Lazarus Phillips.

Paysage (*c.* 1912). 22½ × 28½. S. Saskatoon, Frederick Mendel.

Le Pont. 20 × 26. Montreal, Frederick Kahn.

Reuil, près de Paris. 25½ × 32. Montreal, Mus.

River Landscape with Stormy Sky (*c.* 1918–20). 23½ × 28½. Toronto, A.G.

La Seine à Chatou. 23½ × 28½. S. Ref.: Sauvage, *Vlaminck* (1956), p. 111, Pl. 40. Winnipeg, J. A. MacAulay.

Still Life (1940). 10½ × 8½. S.D. Montreal, Murray Vaughan.

Still Life; Fruit (*c.* 1940). 17 × 21½. S. Saskatoon, Frederick Mendel.

Vase de Fleurs (*c.* 1936). 25 × 21. S. Saskatoon, Frederick Mendel.

Village Street. G., 17½ × 21. S. Toronto, Dr William Landmann.

White House. 13⅜ × 22. Montreal, Frederick Kahn.

ÉDOUARD VUILLARD, 1868–1940

★La Conversation (*c.* 1893). Oil on paper, 19¾ × 24¾. Toronto, A.G.

Fleurs dans un intérieur. B., 15 × 22. S. St Andrews East, Que., Mrs L. T. Porter.

Grand'mère et enfant (1895). 16¼ × 13¼. S. Vancouver, Mrs J. P. Fell.

Interior: Woman at a Table. Oil on paper, 22½ × 16½. S. Montreal, Samuel Bronfman.

Landscape. 16¾ × 23¾. S. Winnipeg, J. A. MacAulay.

La mère de l'artiste. P., 11½ × 10. Montreal, Lazarus Phillips.

La mère de l'artiste (*c.* 1926). 17 × 13¾. S. Ref.: Roger-Marx, *Vuillard* (1945), reprod. p. 29. Vancouver, Mrs J. P. Fell.

Par la fenêtre. B., 14 × 11. S. Montreal, Samuel Bronfman.

Portrait de Cipa Godebsky (*c.* 1895). B., 9⅛ × 8¾. S. Montreal, Mrs I. A. Chipman.

Le Salon de Tristan Bernard (*c.* 1905). 22 × 24¼. S. Ottawa, N.G.C.

Self-portrait in the Studio. B., 10½ × 10. Montreal, Lazarus Phillips.

ITALIAN SCHOOL

GIACOMO BALLA, 1871–1958

Moving Lines (1915). G., 16⅛ × 48. S.D. Toronto, Samuel Zacks.

Pessimism *vs* Optimism (1923). Oil on paper, 25¾ × 21. S. Toronto, Samuel Zacks.

GIORGIO DE' CHIRICO, 1888–

Piazza d'Italia. 9¼ × 13½. S. Toronto, Samuel Zacks.

AMEDEO MODIGLIANI, 1884–1920

★Beatrice Hastings in a Wicker Chair (1915). B., 22 × 18¼. Toronto, Samuel Zacks.

Caryatide. G., 24 × 18½. Toronto, John David Eaton.

Jeune fille. 21½ × 27¾. S. Montreal, Mrs I. A. Chipman.

Portrait de Jeanne Hébuterne. 24⅛ × 15⅛. Ref.: Schaub-Koch, *Modigliani* (1933), reprod. opp. p. 44. Toronto, T. M. Sterling.

Portrait of a Young Woman. 21½ × 15. S. Montreal, Dr S. Graham Ross.

Mme Zborowski. P., 20 × 13½. S. Toronto, D. M. Dunlap.

GINO SEVERINI, 1883–

★Abstract Rhythm of Mme S. (1912). 26¼ × 25½. Toronto, Samuel Zacks.

Black Cat (1911). 21¼ × 28½. S. Ottawa, N.G.C.

Mer-bataille (1915). 19½ × 25¾. Toronto, Samuel Zacks.

View from a Balcony. G., 13½ × 20. S. Fredericton, Beaverbrook A.G.

BELGIAN SCHOOL

JAMES ENSOR, 1860–1949

Jardin d'amour. 25½ × 20½. S. Toronto, Dr William Landmann.

Seascape. 15 × 22½. S. Toronto, Dr William Landmann.

DUTCH SCHOOL

JOHAN BARTHOLD JONGKIND, 1818–1891

Entrée du port de Honfleur (1864). 13¼ × 17. S.D. Ottawa, N.G.C.

Honfleur (1865). W., 11¼ × 14½. S.D. Hamilton, Herman Levy.

Landscape. W., 10 × 16¾. S. Montreal, Oskar Federer.

Landscape with Road (1857?). 16½ × 22. Montreal, P. F. Osler.

Moonlight. 20 × 31¾. Montreal, Mrs D. F. Spotswood.

Moonlight River Landscape (1869). 25½ × 16. S.D. Montreal, P. F. Osler.

Skaters (1862). 16 × 21¼. S.D. Montreal, Miss Olive Hosmer.

View of The Hague (1869). 12⅜ × 17½. S.D. Vancouver, Mrs J. P. Fell.

GERMAN SCHOOL

OTTO DIX, 1891–

★Dr Stadelmann. 37¼ × 26½. Toronto, Dr William Landmann.

Portrait of a Business Man (Josef May). Montreal, Mrs Ghitta Caiserman.

Portrait of a Lawyer (Dr Hugo Simons). P., 39 × 27. S. Montreal, Mrs Hugo Simons.

Woman in a Hat (c. 1920). W., 13¼ × 9½. Saskatoon, Frederick Mendel.

Portrait of Frau Grünebaum (1926). P., 31 × 23½. S. Montreal, Mrs Hugo Simons.

LYONEL FEININGER, 1871–1956

Harbour Bridge (1912). 27½ × 32½. S.D. Saskatoon, Frederick Mendel.

GEORG GROSZ, 1893–1959

Still Life with Bottle and Pipe (1931). 27 × 19½. Toronto, Dr William Landmann.

ERICH HECKEL, 1883–

Grüne Hügel (1917). 26½ × 30½. S.D. Toronto, Dr William Landmann.

Mädchen am Strand (1919). 31 × 27. Montreal, Mrs Hugo Simons.

KARL HOFER, 1878–1955

Head of a Girl. P., 15 × 12½. S. Toronto, Dr William Landmann.

ALEXEI JAWLENSKY, 1864–1941

The Blue Mantilla (1909). 26¾ × 19¼. Toronto, Samuel Zacks.

Lampion. Oil on paper, 16 × 14. S. Ref.: Weiler, *Jawlensky* (1959), No. 247. Montreal, Lazarus Phillips.

Landscape with Trees (c. 1907). 15 × 21¾. S. Ottawa, G. A. Kuay.

Portrait of a Girl (1930). 13 × 10¾. Toronto, David Meltzer.

WASSILY KANDINSKY, 1866–1944

Abstraction (1923). W., 18½ × 16¾. S.D. Toronto, Dr William Landmann.

Red Spearhead (1925). W., 18⅝ × 12⅞. S.D. Toronto, Walter Carsen.

ERNST LUDWIG KIRCHNER, 1889–1938

Father, Mother, and Child (1928). W., 20 × 21½. Saskatoon, Frederick Mendel.

Berghaus (1919). 38 × 28. S.D. Toronto, Dr William Landmann.

PAUL KLEE, 1879–1940

Buntes Distanziert (1923). B., 19¼ × 17. Toronto, Samuel Zacks.

Feuerteufel. 12½ × 9½. Montreal, Dr Paul Dumas.

Figurene Quin (1937). 21¾ × 18. S. Toronto, Samuel Zacks.

Die Idee der Turme (1918). W., 8¾ × 5¾. S.D. Toronto, Samuel Zacks.

Nomaden (1930). W., 9½ × 12½. Montreal, L. V. Randall.

Tierwahn (1930). 14 × 18. S. Toronto, Samuel Zacks.

Topfformen (1921). W., 9 × 7½. S.D. Toronto, Dr William Landmann.

Überwintern (1939). 18 × 34. S. Toronto, Samuel Zacks.

OSKAR KOKOSCHKA, 1886–

★Bordeaux Cathedral (1924–5). 32 × 24. Vancouver, Dr Thomas Ingledow.

MAX LIEBERMANN, 1847–1935

Allée in Wannsee (c. 1912). 28¼ × 36. Saskatoon, Frederick Mendel.

FRANZ MARC, 1880–1916

Pigs (c. 1914). 22¾ × 32¾. S. Saskatoon, Frederick Mendel.

PAULA MODERSOHN-BECKER, 1876–1907

Four Village Children. P., 21 × 15. S. Toronto, Dr William Landmann.

OTTO MÜLLER, 1874–1930

Bathers in a Landscape. 30 × 41. S. Toronto, Dr William Landmann.

EMIL NOLDE, 1867–1956

Head. W., 9½ × 6¼. S. Toronto, Samuel Zacks.

Head of a Girl (1909–12). W., 17 × 14½. S. Saskatoon, Frederick Mendel.

Mary Wigman. W., 18⅞ × 13¾. S. Ottawa, N.G.C.

Still Life with Faience (1915). 28 × 34. S. Toronto, Dr William Landmann.

Still Life with Votive and Iron (1915). 30 × 28. Toronto, Dr William Landmann.

MAX PECHSTEIN, 1881–1955

Landscape with Horse and Rider (1911). 19 × 27. S.D. Toronto, Dr William Landmann.

Still Life with Oranges (1909). 19 × 25. S.D. Toronto, Dr William Landmann.

KARL SCHMIDT-ROTTLUFF, 1884–

Flowers. W., 24 × 19. Winnipeg, Dr Ferdinand Eckhardt.

Grey Landscape in the Taunus. 30 × 39¾. S. Winnipeg, J. A. MacAulay.

★Garten (1919). 28 × 34. Toronto, Dr William Landmann.

Leuchtturm (1913). 25½ × 29. S. Saskatoon, Frederick Mendel.

BRITISH SCHOOL

RICHARD PARKES BONINGTON, 1802–1828

Beach Scene with Figures and Donkeys. 16½ × 9. Montreal, R. W. Reford estate.

Cavalier. 21½ × 24½. Montreal, Mus.

Coast Scene. 12 × 16. S. Ref.: Shirley, *Bonington* (1940), p. 147. Montreal, Mus.

Landscape: a Beach. 9 × 16½. Montreal, R. W. Reford estate.

Landscape with River and Windmill. P., 10½ × 13. Montreal, Mrs William Van Horne.

Landscape with a Wagon (1825). 14½ × 20. Ref.: Shirley, p. 96, Pl. 57. Ottawa, N.G.C.

Landscape with Windmills. Montreal, R. W. Reford estate.

Le Palais des Doges, à Venise (1826). 31½ × 25½. Ref.: Shirley, p. 103. Ottawa, N.G.C.

Scene in Normandy. 20½ × 14. Montreal, R. W. Reford estate.

A Street in Normandy. 15½ × 12. Montreal, P. F. Osler.

Venice: the Grand Canal. 17 × 23¾. Winnipeg, J. A. MacAulay.

View on the South Coast of England. 7¼ × 14½. Montreal, R. W. Reford estate.

View on the South Coast of England. P., 7¼ × 14½. Ref.: Dubuisson, *Bonington* (1924), reprod. opp. p. 63. Montreal, Mus.

★View over the Solent, Isle of Wight. 13½ × 17. Ottawa, R. W. Reford.

SIR EDWARD BURNE-JONES, Bt, 1833–1898

Family Group. 56½ × 44½. Ottawa, G. C. McInnes.

Hero Lighting the Beacon for Leander. Circular, 21 diameter. Sackville, N.B., Mount Allison University.

Mercury and Love, 60¾ × 13. Toronto, University of Toronto.

Portrait of a Girl. 20¾ × 33½. Toronto, University of Toronto.

CHARLES CONDER, 1868–1909

Beach Scene, Boulogne. 15¾ × 23½. Ottawa, N.G.C.

Portrait of Mrs Aikins. 24 × 20. Ottawa, N.G.C.

Woman in a Landscape. 25 × 30. S. Fredericton, Beaverbrook A.G.

WILLIAM ETTY, 1787–1849

A Bivouac of Cupid and his Company. 26 × 36. Ref.: Farr, *Etty* (1958), pp. 139–40, Pl. 69. Montreal, Mus.

Female Nude. B., 27 × 21. Fredericton, Beaverbrook A.G.

Kneeling Nude (attr.). 25⅝ × 18⅜. Ottawa, N.G.C.

Love Triumphant (attr.) (c. 1840–50). 15¼ × 11. S. Montreal, Mus.

Nude with Hand on Head. P., 24 × 20. Fredericton, Beaverbrook A.G.

Reclining Nude. B., 11 × 23¼. Fredericton, Beaverbrook A.G.

Seated Nude (attr.). 24 × 15¾. Ottawa, N.G.C.

Venus and Cupid. 28¼ × 21. Vancouver, A.G.

Venus and her Satellites. W., 9½ × 14½. Ref.: Farr, p. 156. Sackville, New Brunswick, Mount Allison University.

HAROLD GILMAN, 1876–1919

Halifax Harbour (1918). 26¼ × 57. S. Vancouver, A.G.

Halifax Harbour (1918). W., 12 × 20. S. Fredericton, Beaverbrook A.G.

★Halifax Harbour at Sunset (1918). 77 × 132. Ottawa, N.G.C.

Portrait of a Negro. 24 × 20¼. Hamilton, Herman Levy.

The Verandah. 20 × 16. Fredericton, Beaverbrook A.G.

CHARLES GINNER, 1878–1952

The Filling Factory. 120 × 144. Ottawa, N.G.C.

Quayside at Dieppe. 24½ × 17. Edmonton, E. E. Poole.

St Joseph, Highgate (1932). 27 × 20. S. Fredericton, Beaverbrook A.G.

DUNCAN GRANT, 1885–

Acrobats. 30 × 19¾. S. Montreal, Mus.

Farm Pond near Firle, Sussex (1930–2). 31⅜ × 51½. S. Toronto, A.G.

Gladioli (1935). Oil on paper. 40¼ × 30. S.D. Toronto, A.G.

Market Day (1925). 32 × 22¼. S.D. Ottawa, N.G.C.

Mrs Langford (1930). P., 32 × 24. Fredericton, Beaverbrook A.G.

Sunflowers and Dahlias (1932). 29 × 20½. S.D. Hamilton, Herman Levy.

View of the Backs, Cambridge. B., 10½ × 14. Ottawa, N.G.C.

IVON HITCHENS, 1893–

Autumn. 20½ × 41¼. S. Ottawa, N.G.C.

Autumn Arrangement: Right to Left. 16 × 29½. S. Fredericton, Beaverbrook A.G.

Composition (1952). 18 × 42½. S.D. Toronto, John David Eaton.

Composition. 41¼ × 20. Toronto, Mrs A. C. Matthews.

★Forest End. 16 × 29⅜. Ottawa, N.G.C.

Landscape, Sussex. 16 × 43½. Montreal, Mus.

Moorland Pool. 19¾ × 33. S. Vancouver, A.G.

Winter Walk (1948). 20¼ × 41½. S.D. Toronto, A.G.

FRANCES HODGKINS, 1870–1947

Spring in the Ravine. 22¾ × 30. S. Ref.: Howell, *Hodgkins* (1951), p. 108. Ottawa, N.G.C.

The Valley Mill (1930). 25 × 29. S. Ref.: Evans, *Hodgkins* (1948), Pl. 26. Toronto, A.G.

WILLIAM HOLMAN HUNT, 1827–1910

★Henry Wentworth Monk (1858). 20 × 26. Ottawa, N.G.C.

JAMES DICKSON INNES, 1887–1914

Afternoon, Rondda (1913). P., $22\frac{1}{8} \times 30\frac{3}{8}$. S.D. Ref.: Fothergill, *Innes* (1946), P. 28. Toronto, A.G.

Arenig (1911). $14\frac{1}{8} \times 20$. S.D. Ref.: Fothergill, Pl. 17. Ottawa, N.G.C.

Coast Scene (1909). W., $9\frac{5}{8} \times 13\frac{5}{8}$. S.D. Toronto, A.G.

Moorland Landscape with Sunset. 20×20. Winnipeg, J. A. MacAulay.

Pyrénées Orientales. P., $9\frac{1}{4} \times 13$. Vancouver, A.G.

South Wales, Evening. P., 12×10. Ottawa, N.G.C.

AUGUSTUS JOHN, 1879–1961

Aminta (1937). $19\frac{1}{2} \times 12\frac{1}{4}$. S. Ref.: Rothenstein, *John* (1944), Pl. 69. Ottawa, N.G.C.

Canadian Soldier (1917). 32×24. S. Ottawa, N.G.C.

Canadian Soldier (1917). 21×17. Ottawa, N.G.C.

Chiquita. 34×25. S. London, Ont., S. E. Weir.

The Coast Near Antibes. $18\frac{1}{4} \times 21\frac{3}{4}$. S. Toronto, W. E. Phillips.

Cyclamen. $24\frac{1}{4} \times 24\frac{1}{4}$. S. Ref.: *Studio*, cxviii (1939), reprod. p. 145. Ottawa, N.G.C.

Dorelia. $21\frac{1}{8} \times 17$. S. Toronto, W. E. Phillips.

Dorelia. $30 \times 25\frac{1}{8}$. S. Toronto, W. E. Phillips.

Dorelia by the Fence (1910). $19\frac{3}{4} \times 12\frac{1}{2}$. Ref.: Rothenstein, Pl. 15. Port Hope, Ont., The Rt Hon. Vincent Massey.

An Equihen Fisher-girl (*c.* 1900). 18×15. S. Ref.: Rothenstein, p. 20. Ottawa, N.G.C.

Girl in Galway. P., $18\frac{1}{4} \times 13$. S. Toronto, W. E. Phillips.

Girl in Straw Hat. 17×13. Ottawa, N.G.C.

Head of a Girl. 21×17. S. Toronto, W. E. Phillips.

Lady in Black (1917). 34×25. S. Toronto, A.G.

*Marchesa Casati (*c.* 1919). 38×27. Toronto, A.G.

Mrs W. E. Phillips (1951). $47\frac{1}{2} \times 36$. S.D. Toronto, W. E. Phillips.

Nicondera. $20\frac{1}{8} \times 16\frac{1}{8}$. S. Toronto, W. E. Phillips.

Oliver St John Gogarty (1917). 30×25. S.D. Toronto, W. E. Phillips.

Poppet. 21×17. S. Toronto, W. E. Phillips.

Portrait of his Son Edwin. P., $15\frac{3}{4} \times 12\frac{3}{4}$. London, Ont., S. E. Weir.

Portrait Study. $23\frac{1}{2} \times 15\frac{1}{2}$. S. Winnipeg, W. A. Murphy.

Professor Smart. $18\frac{1}{2} \times 15\frac{1}{2}$. Toronto, W. E. Phillips.

Self-portrait. $20\frac{1}{8} \times 16\frac{1}{8}$. S. Ref.: *Connoisseur*, cvi (1940), reprod. p. 35. Ottawa. N.G.C.

Simone (1959). $45\frac{3}{4} \times 35$. S.D. Toronto, W. E. Phillips.

Sir Robert Borden (1919). $36 \times 25\frac{1}{2}$. S.D. Ref.: *International Studio*, lxx (1920), p. 48, reprod. p. 50. Ottawa, N.G.C.

A Summer Noon. P., $16 \times 12\frac{3}{4}$. Ottawa, N.G.C.

T. E. Lawrence as Aircraftman Shaw (1935). $27\frac{3}{4} \times 20\frac{1}{2}$. S. Ref.: *Burlington Magazine*, lxxvii (1940), pp. 133–4, reprod. Ottawa, N.G.C.

Three John Children Wading (*c.* 1909). P., $9\frac{1}{4} \times 13$. Toronto, W. E. Phillips.

Two Women by the Étang de Berre (1910). Ref.: Rothenstein, Pl. 18. Ottawa, Hart Massey.

Vincent Massey. $24\frac{3}{8} \times 20\frac{1}{4}$. S. Ottawa, N.G.C.

W. B. Yeats. 36×28. S. Toronto, W. E. Phillips.

WYNDHAM LEWIS, 1884–1957

Allégresse aquatique (1941). W., $11\frac{1}{2} \times 14\frac{5}{8}$. Toronto, A.G.

The Armada (1937). 36×28. S. Vancouver, A.G.

A Canadian Gun-pit (1918). 121×132. Ottawa, N.G.C.

Lebensraum: the Battlefield (1941). $11\frac{1}{2} \times 16$. S. Toronto, A.G.

The Mud Clinic. $33\frac{1}{2} \times 23$. S. Fredericton, Beaverbrook A.G.

Portrait of J. S. McLean. Toronto, Mrs J. S. McLean.

Portrait of Mrs Paul Martin. Windsor, Ontario, The Hon. Paul Martin.

SIR JOHN MILLAIS, Bt, 1829–1896

The Marquis of Lorne (9th Duke of Argyll) (*c.* 1884). 40×29. Ref.: Millais, *Life and Letters* (1899), ii, pp. 165, 482. Ottawa, N.G.C.

Two Cottage Children. P., $9\frac{1}{2} \times 8$. Sackville, N.B., Mount Allison University.

PAUL NASH, 1889–1946

Chestnut Waters (1924–38). $40\frac{1}{2} \times 50\frac{1}{4}$. S. Ref.: Eates, *Nash* (1948), p. 74, Pl. 43. Ottawa, N.G.C.

Clifton Gorge. W., 15×22. Vancouver, Mrs J. P. Fell.

Cros de Cagnes (1927). 20×30. Fredericton, Beaverbrook A.G.

Dymchurch Steps (1924–44). $26\frac{1}{8} \times 40\frac{1}{8}$. S.D. Ref.: Eates, p. 74, Pl. 26. Ottawa, N.G.C.

Environment for Two Objects. 30×24. Fredericton, Beaverbrook A.G.

Flying Against Germany. 28×38. Ottawa, N.G.C.

Forest of Dean: Study I (1939). W., $15 \times 22\frac{1}{4}$. S. Ref.: Eates, p. 79, Pl. 95. Vancouver, Mrs J. P. Fell.

Landscape of the Crescent Moon (1944). $20\frac{1}{8} \times 29\frac{3}{4}$. S. Ref.: Eates, p. 74. Toronto, A.G.

Landscape of the Red Fungus (1943). W. $15\frac{1}{2} \times 22\frac{1}{2}$. Ref.: Eates, p. 80, Pl. 120. Ottawa, Hart Massey.

Landscape of the Vale. $14\frac{3}{4} \times 22$. Port Hope, Ont., Lionel Massey.

Night Bombardment (1918). 72×84. Ref.: Eates, p. 74. Ottawa, N.G.C.

Nostalgic Landscape: St Pancras Station (*c.* 1930). 25×30. Fredericton, Beaverbrook A.G.

*Solstice of the Sunflower (1945). 28×36. S. Ref.: Eates, p. 79, reprod. in colour, Pl. 115. Ottawa, N.G.C.

Still Life. 36×24. S. Vancouver, Mrs J. P. Fell.

Sunflower. W., 15×22. S. Vancouver, Mrs J. P. Fell.

Vale of the White Blackbird (1943). B., 20×30. S. Ref.: Eates, p. 74. Ottawa, N.G.C.

*Void (1918). 28×36. S. Ref.: Eates, p. 74. Ottawa, N.G.C.

Wooded Landscape (1943). B., 20×30. Ref.: Eates, p. 74. Ottawa, N.G.C.

CHRISTOPHER RICHARD WYNNE NEVINSON, 1889–1946

Returning to the Trenches, 1914. 20×30. S. Ref.: Rothenstein, *Modern English Painters*, ii (1956), p. 139. Ottawa, N.G.C.

The Roads of France. Four panels, each 25 × 67. Ottawa, N.G.C.

War in the Air. 120 × 96. Ottawa, N.G.C.

BEN NICHOLSON, 1894–

Porthmeor Beach, St Ives (1928). 18 × 20¾. S. Edmonton, H. A. Dyde.

Still Life (1948). B., 14½ × 20½. Ref.: Read, *Nicholson*, ii (1956), Pl. 71. Toronto, A.G.

★Still Life: Abelard and Heloise (1950). 47⅛ × 65⅛. Ottawa, N.G.C.

Still Life: Russian Ballet. 25¾ × 17. Vancouver, A.G.

Still Life with Jug (*c.* 1933). 22 × 24. Montreal, Mus.

Zennor Head (1956). B., 20 × 45. Toronto, Harry Davidson.

SIR WILLIAM ORPEN, 1878–1931

A Canadian Airman. 36 × 30. Ottawa, N.G.C.

France: World War (1916). 25 × 30. S. Ref.: Konody and Dark, *Orpen* (1932), p. 98. Fredericton, Beaverbrook A.G.

Field-Marshal Sir Henry Wilson (1919). Ref.: *Orpen* (1923), Pl. 25. St Andrews, N.B., Lady Dunn.

Gen. Sir Arthur Currie. 26 × 30. Ottawa, N.G.C.

Lt.-Gen. Sir Archibald Macdonnell. 26 × 30. Ottawa, N.G.C.

Lottie of Paradise Walk (1908). 36½ × 28½. Ref.: Konody and Dark, p. 194. Ottawa, N.G.C.

Maj.-Gen. Sir Harry Burstall. 36 × 30. Ottawa, N.G.C.

Maj.-Gen. L. J. Lipsett. 36 × 30. Ottawa, N.G.C.

Maj.-Gen. Sir David Watson. 36 × 30. Ottawa, N.G.C.

Maj.-Gen. H. Willis-O'Connor. 36 × 30. Ottawa, N.G.C.

Mary. 23½ × 15½. Ottawa, N.G.C.

President James Loudon. Toronto, University of Toronto.

The Reflection. 35½ × 27½. S. Ottawa, N.G.C.

Richard Barry Fudger (1913). 41½ × 38⅜. Toronto, A.G.

Scene from a Play. 30 × 25. Vancouver, A.G.

Sir F. Loomis. 36 × 30. Ottawa, N.G.C.

The Sketcher: Portrait of Alfred Rich (1910). Ref.: Konody and Dark, p. 219. Toronto, A.G.

W. L. Mackenzie King. 34 × 40. Ottawa, Laurier House.

The Wreck. 19¾ × 24. Fredericton, Beaverbrook A.G.

WILLIAM ROBERTS, 1895–

The First German Gas Attack at Ypres. 120 × 144. Ottawa, N.G.C.

DANTE GABRIEL ROSSETTI, 1828–1882

★Salutatio Beatricis (1859). Two P., each 29½ × 31½. Ottawa, N.G.C.

SIR WILLIAM ROTHENSTEIN, 1872–1945

Harold Jones (1928). 30⅛ × 25. S.D. Ref.: Blake, *Modern English Art* (1937), reprod. p. 47. Ottawa, N.G.C.

Praying Jews (1904). Pastel, 9 × 8½. S.D. Ottawa, N.G.C.

The Watch on the Rhine: The Last Phase. Ref.: *Rothenstein* (1923), Pl. 26. Ottawa, N.G.C.

JOHN SINGER SARGENT, 1856–1925

Joseph Joachim. 34½ × 28¾. S. Ref.: Charteris, *Sargent* (1927), p. 278. Toronto, A.G.

Pressing the Grapes: a Florentine Wine Cellar. 24 × 20. Fredericton, Beaverbrook A.G.

San Vigilio, Lake Garda (1913). 28 × 72. Ref.: Charteris, p. 292. Fredericton, Beaverbrook A.G.

Viscount Byng of Vimy (1922). 22 × 15½. S. Ref.: Charteris, p. 276. Ottawa, N.G.C.

WALTER RICHARD SICKERT, 1860–1942

Au Caboulet au bout du quai (*c.* 1920). 24 × 20. S. Ref.: Browse, *Sickert* (1960), p. 87. Montreal, Mus.

Blackmail: Mrs Barrett (*c.* 1908). Pastel, 26 × 21¼. S. Ref.: Browse, p. 87. Ottawa, N.G.C.

The Blue Corset (1912). 21 × 18¼. Hamilton, Herman Levy.

Bonne fille (*c.* 1903). 17½ × 14½. S. Ref.: Browse, p. 87. Fredericton, Beaverbrook A.G.

Café des Tribunaux, Dieppe (1890). 26¾ × 20. Ref.: Browse, pp. 63, 87, Pl. 8. Ottawa, N.G.C.

Christine. Pastel. 24 × 15. Edmonton, E. E. Poole.

Corner of Rue Notre-Dame, and the Arcades de la Poissonnerie (1900). 15½ × 12½. S.D. Ref.: Browse, pp. 66, 86. Fredericton, Beaverbrook A.G.

Cumberland Market (*c.* 1898). 16 × 20. S. Ref.: Browse, p. 88. Toronto, A.G.

Façade of Saint-Jacques, Dieppe (1902). 21½ × 18. Ref.: Browse, p. 67. Hamilton, Herman Levy.

King Edward VIII (1937). 72 × 36. S. Ref.: Browse, pp. 21, 87. Fredericton, Beaverbrook A.G.

Lady Dunn. St Andrews, N.B., Lady Dunn.

Lansdown Crescent, Bath (1916–18). P., 10 × 8. S. Ref.: Browse, pp. 79, 87, Pl. 79. Fredericton, Beaverbrook A.G.

Lansdown Crescent, Bath: Mr Sheepshanks' House (1916–18). P., 10 × 8. S. Ref.: Browse, p. 87. Fredericton, Beaverbrook A.G.

Marie and Hubby. 18½ × 15. Hamilton, A.G.

★The Old Bedford: Cupid in the Gallery (*c.* 1890). 50 × 30½. Ottawa, N.G.C.

The Old Middlesex (*c.* 1890). 25 × 30. S. Ref.: Browse, p. 86. Fredericton, Beaverbrook A.G.

Rue Notre-Dame, Dieppe (*c.* 1902). 52 × 41⅝. S. Ref.: Browse, pp. 66, 87. Ottawa, N.G.C.

Saint-Jacques, Dieppe, the Façade (*c.* 1900). S. Ref.: Browse, p. 88. Toronto, A.G.

Sir James Dunn, Bt (1934). 72 × 24. S. Ref.: Browse, pp. 21, 87. St Andrews, N.B., Lady Dunn.

Sunday Afternoon (*c.* 1912). 20 × 12. S. Ref.: Browse, p. 87. Fredericton, Beaverbrook A.G.

Viscount Castlerose (*c.* 1933). 82 × 27½. S. Ref.: Browse, pp. 21, 87. Fredericton, Beaverbrook A.G.

SIR MATTHEW SMITH, 1879–1959

Approaching Storm, Cagnes. 12½ × 18. S. London, Ont., S. E. Weir.

Bouquet of Flowers. 20 × 16. S. Vancouver, Mrs J. P. Fell.

★Bouquet of Flowers. 26 × 21¾. Ottawa, N.G.C.

Flowers. 32 × 23½. Ottawa, Hart Massey.

Landscape, Fréjus (c. 1938–9). 18⅛ × 21⅜. Ottawa, N.G.C.

Near Lyon (1922). 12½ × 18. S. London, Ont., S. E. Weir.

Pears against a Red Background (1947). 36 × 28½. Fredericton, Beaverbrook A.G.

Portrait of Augustus John (1945). 30 × 25. Montreal, Mus.

Reclining Nude (c. 1925). 19¾ × 28¾. Ottawa, N.G.C.

Reclining Nude, No. 1. 19¾ × 28¾. Fredericton, Beaverbrook A.G.

Still Life Arrangement, No. 2. 32 × 32. Montreal, Mus.

Still Life at Fryern, No. 1 (1944). Ottawa, N.G.C.

Still Life with Two Jugs (1938). 31¾ × 23⅝. S. Toronto, A.G.

Tulips (c. 1938–9). 28⅜ × 19¼. Ottawa, N.G.C.

White Dahlias and Pears. 32 × 25¼. Ottawa, Hart Massey.

Woman Seated (c. 1913). 22⅜ × 18¾. Ottawa, N.G.C.

SIR STANLEY SPENCER, 1891–1959

Alpine Landscape. 23¼ × 35. Vancouver, A.G.

The Jubilee Tree (1936). 36 × 29¾. Ref.: Rothenstein, *Spencer* (1945), Pl. 50. Toronto, A.G.

Magnolia at Odney Club (1938). 36⅛ × 24⅛. Ref.: Rothenstein, Pl. 67. Ottawa, N.G.C.

The Marriage at Cana (1953). 36 × 60. Fredericton, Beaverbrook A.G.

★Marsh Meadow, Cookham. 25 × 30. Ottawa, N.G.C.

Miss Elizabeth Winperis (1939). 30 × 22. Ref.: Rothenstein, Pl. 75. Ottawa, N.G.C.

The Resurrection: Rejoicing (1946). Three panels, each 30 × 20. Fredericton, Beaverbrook A.G.

Self-portrait (1944). B., 15¾ × 11½. Ottawa, N.G.C.

PHILIP WILSON STEER, 1860–1942

The Edge of the Cliff, Bridgenorth (1901). 38 × 40. S. Ref.: MacColl, *Steer* (1945), p. 203. Ottawa, N.G.C.

Gathering Seaweed, Harwich (1913–32). 24⅛ × 36. S.D. Ref.: Ironside, *Steer* (1943), Pl. 62. Ottawa, N.G.C.

Lady Playing Patience. Qualicum Beach, B.C., H. R. Milner.

The Limekiln (1908). 18 × 24. S.D. Ref.: MacColl, p. 210. Ottawa, N.G.C.

Maldon (1920). 18 × 30. S.D. Ref.: MacColl, p. 218. Fredericton, Beaverbrook A.G.

On the Plage (1892). P., 8 × 10⅛. S. Ref.: MacColl, p. 193. Fredericton, Beaverbrook A.G.

Portrait: the Artist's Model (1921). 24 × 20¼. Ref.: MacColl, p. 219. Ottawa, N.G.C.

The Thames at Chelsea, Sunset (1923). 16 × 24. S.D. Ref.: MacColl, p. 220. Ottawa, N.G.C.

The Valley of the Severn (1902). 26¼ × 36¼. S. Ref.: Ironside, Pl. 36. Ottawa, N.G.C.

EDWARD WADSWORTH, 1889–1949

Dazzle-ships in Drydock at Liverpool. 120 × 96. Ottawa, N.G.C.

Honfleur. P., 25⅛ × 35. Ref.: *Studio*, cxxv (1943), p. 173. Ottawa, N.G.C.

The Jetty, Fécamp. P., 25 × 35. Fredericton, Beaverbrook A.G.

DAME ETHEL WALKER, 1861–1951

Gabriel van Schnell. 30 × 25. S. Ottawa, N.G.C.

Lady in Blue. 30 × 25. Ottawa, N.G.C.

GEORGE FREDERICK WATTS, 1817–1904

Ellen Terry. 29½ × 17½. Vancouver, Mrs Jonathan Rogers.

Time, Death, and Judgement. 96 × 65½. Ref.: Watts, *Watts* (1912), ii, p. 215. Ottawa, N.G.C.

JAMES McNEILL WHISTLER, 1834–1903

Lillie in our Alley (c. 1898). 20½ × 12½. Ottawa, N.G.C.

Reclining Woman. P., 8¼ × 10¾. S. Montreal, Mrs Howard W. Pillow.